QUINTON'S LEGACY

Quinton's Legacy

ISBN 978-0-9863442-9-9

www.quintonsmessages.com

Cover design by Red Zen

Book design by Bella Media Management

Printed in the United States of America.

First Edition

"It has been a great joy to work with Ernie and Kristine Jackson on his latest book: Quinton's Legacy. The Jacksons have experienced the worst yet expect the best of life. When I've been with them, an unexplainable sense of joy and hope overtakes me and I know they are destine to help a great many people with their stories of courage, forgiveness and eagerness to understand the truth. This book is a journey of their personal discoveries and spiritual awakening. With a passion to help others, they open their lives to us, shining a light of hope. Their leadership is a healing balm so necessary for our world today. You will be blessed in a hundred ways when you read this book."

Jan M. Whalen, MASL
Whalen Voices, LLC

"When I read Quinton's Messages, I was moved by how devastating and life-changing that one moment was for the Jackson family, yet they chose forgiveness. This is a huge lesson for us all. I couldn't wait to read Ernie's second book Quinton's Legacy. Again, I couldn't put the book down and was fascinated by his stories of personal growth.

Quinton's Legacy is an amazing resource, a learning tool, for those who are just beginning their spiritual path. Ernie explains his own learning curve in such an easy to understand, everyday way. This message is vital and it's clear to me that this book will help many people understand that our loved ones never leave us, and they show us signs all the time. Well done, Ernie. I look forward to book number three."

Laurie Savoie
Author of *The Ripple Effect: Invisible Impact of Suicide*

"Quinton's Legacy is a very touching, and an emotional book. Ernie writes so very well it is hard to put the book down, I couldn't wait to find out what was next. The stories he shared of others tragic losses and the true spiritual and psychic encounters they shared were amazing and very healing for many of us who have had such losses. It gives us hope. For me I loved seeing how many different people with similar circumstances regardless of religion or belief systems had the same psychic-spiritual, and healing experience. So many of us don't want to talk about this "stuff" as people will think I'm weird etc... it's time we talk about it. This book does just that.

I highly recommend this book for anyone experiencing loss or those who are curious about the other side."

Psychic-Medium, Dave Campbell
Owner of the Astrology Store in Glendale, Arizona

QUINTON'S LEGACY

ERNIE JACKSON

DEDICATION

Dedicated to our son Quinton Stone Jackson for loving me so much that he sacrificed himself to open my eyes. Also dedicated to everyone grieving the loss of a loved one; may you know that they still exist, and that you will, too.

ACKNOWLEDGMENTS

I don't know who I would have become without my wife Kristine Cano Jackson. She continues to stand by me through better or worse, with patience and love. Thank you for your love, kindness and patience with me. To my daughter Cheyanne Eve Jackson, the first one who opened my eyes wide to what is truly important. Sweetheart, please forgive me for losing my way. My son Quinton Stone Jackson, thank you for everything. I am sorry we had to do this again, and I pray I don't lose my way once more. Don't lose faith in me son, as I move toward a consistent rise in my vibration so I may sense you more frequently. To my son-in-law Salvador, thank you for loving my daughter and for your kindness, patience and love. With you as her husband, I know she is safe. To our Bubbles, our grandson Salvador Quinton, thank you for the joy and silliness you bring out in me.

Thank you to my friends and fellow authors Dave Campbell, Mark Kilburn, and Laurie Savoie for reading the preliminary manuscripts, providing your thoughtful feedback, and most of all, encouragement to finally get this book finished. Thank you Mark Ireland for an amazing Foreword.

I was looking for a spiritual person with knowledge and knowhow to take our work and polish it, then bring it to the light of day. Thank you to our friend and author Anne Puryear for making the connection to Jan Whalen. Jan, thank you for collaborating with us, helping us to hone the sharing of our experiences and others, our thoughts and our philosophies. Your work on this project was amazing; I really should give you a byline! Thank you for bringing Quinton's Legacy to the light of day.

Thank you, mom and dad – Frances and Ernest James Jackson (Darden) – for being my parents and laying the groundwork for who I am today. Thank you to my in-laws Ed and Nellie Cano for showing me the way. To my sisters Regina and Tina: thank you picking me to be your big brother; I did the best I could to help, but I was only a child myself. To my nieces, Kylie, Jordan, and Jacqueline: I am so proud of the young women you have become. To my nephews, TK and Alex: thank you for being part of my life; you are like sons to me. To all my friends and acquaintances, I will not start naming names because I know I would forget someone. To all of you, thank you for being part of my life, for encouraging me to be the best me, for restoring me when I was down, listening to me when I felt the need to share, and celebrating our return to the living. To those of you from the Evergreen High School class of 1983, thank you for getting us home after the accident and getting me involved with the football team. You know who you are; I am eternally grateful. Thank you to Coach Molholm (Senior and Junior) for letting me be part of the current Evergreen High School football program; it means more to me than you know. To my people in the Conifer and Evergreen foothill communities in Colorado: you nursed us back to health and lifted us during every step of our journey. To our friends and family in Arizona: thank you for all your love and support. To my east coast family: thank you for being there for us; I wish we could spend more time together. I keep saying I have to go back east for a visit, but life gets in the way. All I can say is–I will! Thank you all for continuing to be part of our journey and watching out for us.

TABLE OF CONTENTS

FOREWORD

Your child just died and you are in a state of utter shock. You can't breathe, eat, or sleep. You hurt from head to toe and you're hoping that this is a horrible dream from which you will soon wake.

After a while you realize that in some ways this is all a dream — this temporal world is but one aspect of a much larger reality. With this new perspective you are suddenly compelled to express gratitude for what you have, to forgive others, to honor your child, and to share your truth rather than being angry and secluding yourself. In taking this course you are healed and transformed. You've been endowed with a gift that provides you with strength you didn't know you had. You grow in wisdom and are compelled to share it with others. This is now your duty and also your passion.

What I just described is the life path of Ernie Jackson, the author of this book. Ernie and I have both experienced something no parent wants to go through — the loss of a child. From an earthly perspective, Ernie's son, Quinton and my youngest son, Brandon both passed "prematurely." But what makes us so sure that this common way of viewing things is correct? Who is to say when it is our time to go and why should we think that the expected order is necessarily the natural or correct one?

Ernie and I met several years ago and became instant friends — perhaps more like brothers. There was an instant bond between us, founded in mutual respect and appreciation for one another. Yes, we had both lost sons but we had even more in common than that.

I believe there are three reasons why Ernie asked me to write a Foreword to this book. First, my role as a partner, with Elizabeth Boisson in co-founding "Helping Parents Heal"—an organization created to assist bereaved parents. Ernie has been very involved with HPH and has personally seen the healing effect this platform has provided to grieving parents.

Next, I am the son of Richard Ireland, a prominent 20th Century Minister who happened to be very psychic too. In addition to his time behind a pulpit my father counseled celebrities like Mae West, Amanda Blake, and Glenn Ford and was even acquainted with the Eisenhower's. But most importantly from my perspective, he gave me proof that life doesn't cease with physical death—our spiritual essence carries on. Many of us hope for his, but he knew it and I came to know it too.

Finally, I have conducted research and uncovered convincing evidence for the afterlife, publishing two books on the subject. In Soul Shift and Messages from the Afterlife I share compelling personal experiences and also relay the scientific case for life after death.

Over the past eleven years I've met many parents who have experienced the excruciating pain of losing a child. Among these individuals, I've found that women are typically more open to expressing their emotions than men, embracing the pain and simultaneously opening themselves up to the healing process.

I've also found that women are usually more open to considering the possibility that the spiritual essence of their child lives on—and may make contact with them in a variety of ways. These experience help soothe their grief, giving them hope to carry on and lead productive, happy lives.

Men are often more guarded with their emotions and many are more skeptical when it comes to spiritual matters. But there is nothing like losing a child to open a person's mind to greater possibilities and Ernie Jackson serves as an excellent example in this regard. The passing of his beloved son, Quinton changed Ernie in ways previously unimaginable to him or his family. Ernie was shell-shocked by this experience, but it stretched and molded him into someone new — the person he was always destined to be. He has embraced this truth.

Not every parent can move forward at the pace Ernie did and some will be engulfed by grief and anger for some time to come. Sharing his wisdom about this Ernie states, "We are not to judge or compare our experiences, our individual journeys." This is such an important point, because many of us are tempted to compare our path with what other people experience, leading to judgment. When we stop comparing, we stop judging and start loving. This is the essence of true compassion.

In working with bereaved parents, both independently and through Helping Parents Heal, I've spoken about what I term the "four pillars of healing." These pillars are things I've observed and taken inventory of, involving parents who have moved forward with healthy, fulfilling lives.

The first pillar is for the bereaved individual to receive loving support from friends and family. We all need someone to lean on who truly cares about us at a time of grief and many of us are blessed with such support. Unfortunately some people won't have this resource, but that's where the second pillar can come in.

The second pillar is about the grieving person meeting and developing relationships with other parents who have been through the same thing. No one can relate to a bereaved parent, or empathize with them like another parent who has lost a child. The second pillar can be especially helpful for the newly bereaved when they meet a parent who has been able to move forward in a positive way. Ernie exemplifies this and actually displayed these positive characteristics much more quickly than what most would consider a "normal" timeframe.

The third pillar is for the bereaved person to be of service to others — when they are ready for this. When you help others heal, you are also healed. I've seen this many times before and it is a marvelous thing. Service can be anything that feels right to the individual. Many parents set up foundations for their children, raising funds to aid causes related to their child that passed. Others donate time to worthwhile causes, or just reach out to help other people through daily interactions. Ernie is an example of a person who has provided service to others in a variety of ways, perhaps most importantly by sharing his truth.

The fourth pillar, which differentiates Helping Parents Heal from other organizations, is openness to exploring and considering evidence for life after death. This is the hope pillar and I've seen it make a big difference in people's lives. As Ernie notes in his books, he never gave any thought to the notion of an afterlife before Quinton passed, but now feels compelled to shout it from the rooftops. Ernie has experienced compelling proof of Quinton's ongoing existence, including direct contact. People are truly healed when they come to understand that there really is a spiritual realm and physical death is not the end.

And I think Ernie has shown me that there is also a fifth pillar that deserves some attention, which is forgiveness. When we forgive others and ourselves the door is opened for the possibility of healing. When we hold onto anger and self-judgment it just hurts us and prolongs our suffering.

Ernie Jackson embodies someone who has successfully navigated the murky and turbulent waters of grief, coming out strong and whole. He is now the person he was always destined to be – a teacher and a healer. I encourage you to listen to Ernie's heartfelt truth and prepare to be transformed.

Mark Ireland

SUMMARY OF *QUINTON'S MESSAGES*

My first book, *Quinton's Messages,* tells the story of our family before and after the car accident that took the life of our nine-year-old son Quinton. I share my journey, my awakening, as I begin to deal with the grief of losing a child. As impossible as it seemed at the time, Quinton revealed himself to us in a variety of ways, and our contact with him convinced my wife Kristine and me that *there is more* to this existence and, most importantly, there is no death. We were being led down the rabbit hole, as they say.

We refer to Quinton's death as a "transition" because he showed us that even though he doesn't have a physical body, he is still alive. He is with us. In short, *Quinton's Messages* celebrates Quinton's memory and then tells the story of the journey of my awakening.

Before Quinton's transition, I was lost. I was absorbed in the pursuit of material wealth, acquiring possessions and racing towards an empty destination; a fruitless endeavor at best. Ultimately, with Quinton's guidance, I now understand that the journey is the *only thing* that matters.

At its core, *Quinton's Messages* was designed to open the reader's eyes by sharing my story. I was someone whose eyes were closed. Before his death, I sensed a change. I thought something new was coming, but I ignored that thought-somehow thinking it could be controlled. After his transition, there were many "aha" moments (as I came to call them). These moments of coincidence, synchronicities and elevated levels of consciousness led me toward a different vision of reality--one that I'm passionate to share with others.

This journey was filled with awe. The expansion of my perception of life in general found its way into the book. While it was my journey, many of the readers of *Quinton's Messages* identified with what the book conveyed. It is unfortunate that my son had to "die" at such a young age. Yet this transition, this ultimate "Oh My God" moment, was the catalyst for something I can only call the ultimate gift.

The book describes how Quinton came through to Kristine and me—to our awe and amazement. I just didn't know it was even possible. When I look back at the programs we used to watch (even before Quinton was born) like "Touched by An Angel," "Ghost Whisperer" and "It's a Wonderful Life," I used to think they were simply motivational entertainment. Never, ever did I consider there might be any reality in them.

When Quinton began to visit, it was over the top for us. Yet when we reported our new reality, and as we shared our stories, others told similar stories of their loved ones' visits. Many verified our own experiences, so I included them in the book.

Because of Quinton's transition, on a certain level, life improved. This is a very bitter pill to swallow. I truly don't recommend telling anyone who has just "lost" a loved one that some good may come out of that loss. It's just too soon, and they are not ready to hear this message. There just isn't any good way to say that, and I don't know if the time is ever right. My experience gives me direct proof that good can come to us through a tragic event.

Because of my son's transition, I became an assistant football coach at Evergreen High School, my alma mater. Because of my son, I had the courage to accept the nomination to be president of the Denver BOMA (Buildings Owners and Managers Association) chapter. Because of my son, *Quinton's Messages* was written. All of these examples impact hundreds in various ways. None of this would have happened because I lacked the courage, conviction and passion to make it so. We were pleasantly surprised when a dear friend came to me after reading the book and said, "Do you have any idea how many messages are in this book?"

On the deepest level, *Quinton's Messages* illustrates that any of us – all of us – do not have to be defined by the adversity we have faced; whether it's abuse or neglect, death or disease. Any of us – all of us – can courageously face whatever adversity life has in store. We can turn our challenges around with strength and rise above the cycle.

Quinton's Legacy, the second book of the series, is the continuing story of our journey. There is something for anyone willing to go a little deeper into the rabbit hole with us.

INTRODUCTION

So much has happened since the publication of Quinton's Messages. Much of it is amazing and all of it with purpose. The journey has continued and, while the extraordinary has become commonplace, I still want more. More visits, more signs, more sharing of our message!

My friend, John McDonough, who is a poet, photographer and philosopher, and my wife Kristine helped me crystalize the message I share with people who have lost a loved one or are searching for greater meaning in life. I use it in my standard signature for Quinton's Messages: "What we are dealing with is not a matter of believing or a belief. We are dealing with knowledge; know there is more!"

This book, Quinton's Legacy, is the sequel and written primarily for those who read the first book. Quinton's Legacy has three sections.

The first section is the story of our journey to forgiveness, Quinton's visits with us, messages from Quinton via renowned medium Rebecca Rosen, discovering my guardian angel and reconciliation with my deceased father. We continue to discover what "there is more" means for us.

Section two includes stories from others who have experienced visits from deceased loved ones—messages from beyond the grave. We also discovered that when our pets transition, it is possible for them to be here for us also. Now that the door has been opened, the revelations that once filled me with awe, amazement and reverence have become the norm; my eyes are opened to how the world works. If these ideas are new to you, buckle your seat belts. You are about to go for a ride.

Section three provides practical advice. We go beyond merely reporting the divine experiences that have blessed us to share a broader perspective; a snapshot of what I have come to believe. You see, in opening the door to there is more, all of us are invited to learn and embrace new ways of thinking about life and death. I share my perspective, in general terms, from our family's experiences since Quinton's transition, as well as from those who have crossed our paths. We note multiple sources to further illustrate that these experiences are not unique; they occur so frequently that they're commonplace.

Yes, what we have experienced is an amazing peek inside the workings of the universe. With that said, the purpose of Quinton's Messages, and this sequel, is to pique your interest enough to do your own research. The experiences we share, along with this information, can be found from the Internet, bookshelves or firsthand. All that is required is to slow down from time to time and take note of what you are experiencing, and then acknowledge it for what it is.

Enjoy the journey and in knowing *there is more*.

Section One

Our Journey Continues

Chapter One

THE CROSS

Quinton's Lesson: There are no coincidences!

A man and a woman walk into a store at approximately 3:00 p.m. on July 10, 2009. The man is a Nazi paraphernalia collector and definitely not religious, but something catches his eye. He stepped into the store looking for something to add to his collection, not knowing what he was looking for. He picked up this shiny piece of metal; it was actually surgical steel. He turned it over in his hands marveling at it. The woman with him looked at him with a perplexed expression wondering why he'd be interested in something like that.

He continued to examine it. It is strong and bright, reflecting the light of the sun's rays. The two pieces of surgical steel were held together by an Allen bolt. The woman grew even more perplexed as it appeared that the man was going to purchase this item, which definitely is not a piece of Nazi paraphernalia. He made the purchase and the woman asked, "What are you doing?" He shrugged his shoulders, "I really don't know." But he had purchased the cross in spite of himself.

This man, like any other, has his good traits and less-than-desirable traits. He is not a Godly man, but he took care of this woman in an astounding way when her world turned upside down. He cooks for her, cleans for her and is handy around the house. At one point, they even

1

considered getting married, but that was before his less-than-desirable attributes revealed themselves.

They arrived home still not having a clue as to why he purchased the cross or what he would do with it. On this eventful day, a nightmare was about to unfold. After shopping, they went home to rest because he was recovering from knee surgery, and this was the day of his follow-up exam. His knee was badly infected; his regiment of antibiotics and anti-inflammatory medications was beginning, and he was worn out.

The woman was tired too, so both napped for about two hours. Around 7:00 p.m. the phone rang. It was her mom. "Regina," she heard through frantic tears, "There's been an accident." This was the accident that took the life of Quinton Stone Jackson. Regina fell apart, because Quinton was her nephew. The man held it together providing sound counsel, helping Regina to think rationally.

After insisting that Regina sleep, he tried to sleep too. The following day, June 11, after making arrangements for a friend of the family to watch Regina's three children, they picked up our mom at McCarran International Airport in Las Vegas and then drove 12 torturous hours. They finally arrived in Farmington, New Mexico. During the drive, he gently reminded Regina to slow down; one accident is quite enough for the family.

When they arrived at my room, I let them in. I was grateful to see them. Later, they told me that they'll be forever haunted by the expression on my face. I was a shell of a man at that moment. I was alone and, in heartbreaking silence, dealing with the death of my son. My wife Kristine Cano-Jackson was in the ICU for her second night. I had spent the first night with her, and then Nellie, her mother, my daughter Cheyanne and Cheyanne's best friend Layla would take turns on subsequent nights. So when my sister, mom and my sister's boyfriend arrived, I was utterly shattered and alone.

Quinton's Legacy

They arrived exhausted and fearful. They just didn't know what to expect, but they knew that we needed them, and they needed to be with us. After hugs and tears, they gave me the once-over and were horrified at the sight of my leg. Regina and her boyfriend left immediately for medical supplies while I sat with Mom, trying to begin the process of understanding what had happened to our family and coming to terms with the death of my son. When they came back, they cleaned my wounds.

Two or three months later, while we visited them in Las Vegas, the man gave me the cross saying, "I think I bought this for you." This cross was purchased about two-and-one-half hours before my son transitioned. It is impossible to attempt to explain this away as coincidence.

I have come to believe that any of us, at any time, can get tapped on the shoulder by God and told to do something. When this happens, it's best to follow that feeling; be an angel for another person. This man did that for me and my family. Not one of us is exempt from that ultimate tap on the shoulder, regardless of how our society has labeled us or even what we think of ourselves. In these instances, the judgment we heap on others and ourselves is meaningless.

While I have struggled with organized religion my whole life, I have found comfort in the words of Christ. His teachings are echoed through time across many religions, faiths and beliefs. What a shame that humankind has allowed itself to be divided over what name we use for God and how to worship, talk and what to believe. What a shame. For those who denounce religion, naming the millions who have been killed in the name of a religion, I get it – believe me. My response will always be the same. This isn't the work of God, it's the misguided work of mankind.

Things ended quite badly for Regina and her boyfriend, but I will be forever grateful that he acted on his feelings that day. Maybe his angel, or God, whispered in his mind. But the important thing is that he let his inner voice guide him. I continue to wear the cross today. It reminds me that God uses all of us. For me, it is a symbol of hope.

Chapter Two

FORGIVENESS

Quinton's Lesson: Forgiveness is from the heart, not the mind!

Throughout my late teens, there were times I drove with suicidal resolve. It wasn't that I was truly suicidal, but my life was joyless. The violence and fear at home, being painfully shy and not really knowing how to enjoy myself or my life, added up to feeling that I didn't fit in. I didn't date and didn't party as I walked through life in a self-created isolation.

The one thing I did enjoy was driving—the faster the better! I did some awfully stupid things. Once, I drove on a county road in the fog at 120 mph. I took a 45 mph curve at 125 mph – on tires so bald that the steel belted radials were showing. I even turned left at a busy intersection while the light was red, and these are just a few I remember.

Each time I did stupid things like this, I knew the consequences. My mantra during my risky driving was: "Please don't let me take anybody with me." It was a heartfelt prayer. The mere thought of being responsible for the death of another would make my soul shudder; it was my worst nightmare. Yet when I was taking chances with my driving, I would actually ask the question, "Is today the day for me to die?"

All these thoughts flashed through my mind as I looked up at Amanda, the woman who caused the accident, as she looked down at me and my dying son Quinton. No words were spoken. Through the grief in her eyes, the expression of utter horror on her face and in her soul, I saw it all. She felt responsible for the death of our son.

As I lay there with Quinton, in the brief moment when our eyes met, I immediately forgave Amanda. She was living *my* nightmare; her grief was my grief. In that instance, she was me. Given my past, forgiving her was the only natural reaction. I didn't have to think about it, meditate on it or let it come to me over time. It was immediate. I am not sure how this is possible, but this is the way it happened for me. I do believe that this immediate feeling of forgiveness in my heart for Amanda made it possible for Quinton to make contact so quickly with me. It was different for my wife. Kristine went through the gamut of emotions – from screaming for revenge and justice in the emergency room after learning that Quinton was dead to forgiving Amanda – but it took months. A legal resolution for the case took two long years.

When the investigator arrived in Conifer to interview us over the summer of 2010, a full year after the accident, I still wasn't sure how Kristine felt. We met Special Agent Troy Cook at Wendy's in Conifer at 4:30 one afternoon. I raced up the hill from my job as an assistant property manager at Independence Plaza to meet Kristine and the investigator. Special Agent Cook worked for the Bureau of Indian Affairs – Ute Mountain Agency based in Towaoc, Colorado. As we sat there with him, talking and slowly becoming more comfortable with each other, our conversation loosened up. He eventually shared that he had a very high success rate on the cases he worked. His success was measured by the fact that those found guilty, in his cases, were punished to the maximum extent allowable by law. Knowing that I had already forgiven Amanda, I began to be a little concerned over his success rate.

I knew I had to explain to him that I wanted the court to be lenient with Amanda. While Kristine and I had begun to discuss asking the court for leniency, we really hadn't finalized our discussion in the matter. As I started talking about leniency, I looked to my left at Kristine to judge the expression on her face and was relieved to see that she didn't disagree. The investigator seemed surprised, but he took notes and the meeting ended.

Yes, Kristine and I forgave differently, just as Kristine and I grieved differently. It's best not to judge the differences in our experiences, that much is clear. This is a fine point I discovered, a point that often results in angry misunderstandings and divorce for couples. We are not to judge or compare our experiences, our individual journeys. They are what they are. Our task is to understand and be compassionate with one another as we walk through that hell. Just because I forgave Amada first doesn't make me a "good" person. Kristine needed time to process this event on her own timeline. As it applies to Kristine and me, it applies to us all.

For me, it relates more to the energy we create, project and attract back to ourselves. The difference is between walking around angry at the world and judging others who don't see eye to eye with us. To me, it's better to simply accept that we are all souls along the same path, but at different points along that path. The difference between forgiveness and judgment is the difference between being compassionate and not compassionate. While this may seem like an oversimplification, the energy created by the contradictory approach is vastly different. It not only dramatically alters our individual perspectives of life but what we attract back into our lives.

As far as the court case is concerned, not much happened for the first six months after the accident, but we were concerned about Amanda without even knowing her yet. Later, we learned that Amanda and her family felt the same about us. The justice system and insurance system, in cases like ours, are very well organized and protective of both parties. Simultaneously, and on multiple occasions, both parties tried to make contact. We were unsuccessful. Both of us tried to utilize our respective insurance companies to make contact. When I spoke to theirs, I implored them to give Amanda the message that we didn't bear her any ill will. She didn't get this message. Meanwhile, they were working with their insurance agent with the instruction not to slow down their process.

As the New Year arrived, January 2011, the pace of the case began to increase. Court documents were issued with all of our names included. We began talking to Carol Morris, a victim's advocate, and Todd Norvell, assistant district attorney, again reiterating our desire for the court to be lenient with Amanda. Amanda's family now knew who we were and, unbeknownst to us, began researching on the Internet in an effort to find out more about us. They quickly found the vimeo.com video recorded July 29, 2009 when I shared that fateful day and watched it several times. Amanda's mental anguish multiplied, so she could not watch the video. But her parents told her about it, especially the part about the medicine man. We found out later that her deceased grandfather, who had transitioned 10 years prior, was a medicine man!

The State of Colorado charged Amanda with three misdemeanors, two of which were reckless driving, resulting with serious physical injury, and one reckless driving resulting in death. Because there were no alcohol or drugs involved, felony charges didn't apply. For each charge, Amanda could face a maximum sentence of one year, for a total of three years. We knew it just didn't matter since we wished for leniency. Serving jail time – any jail time – seemed pointless to us in this case, as we knew the sentence she was already serving was a heavy load. Poor Amanda was walking around carrying her own sentence of feeling responsible for the death of a child, our child. We felt that after that, jail time would be a waste of time and do more harm to her soul than good.

During the first quarter of 2011, we worked with both the assistant district attorney and victim's advocate, even meeting with her in her office in Denver, all for the purpose of finding a way to minimize Amanda's jail time. We said it often and, as a result of our persistence, the assistant district attorney reached out to us asking permission to drop the two reckless driving resulting with serious physical injury charges.

Naturally we agreed, leaving one year on the table with the court and the case. But one year behind bars still seemed counterproductive to us. Looming over us was the thought of the lead investigator's comments of always achieving a maximum sentence for his cases. We turned our attention to the last remaining charge relating to Quinton's death.

As this process continued, we let the victim's advocate know that we intended to be present in court during sentencing. A court date was set for the beginning of the second quarter of 2011. The court date was one year and 51 weeks from the date of Quinton's passing – essentially two years. This is no coincidence, and it isn't at all ironic. We feel it was intended by God. Also, we were scheduled to be in the town where the court was to convene, on our way to celebrate Quinton and Ed's life (my father-in-law who passed June 8, 2003) in Rocky Point, Mexico. We let the victim's advocate know that date would work out for us and continued to advocate verbally for no jail time. Late in April, we received our opportunity to put our perspective into a formal court document. We were provided a victim's advocacy statement, which is shown here. The bolded black print is what the document asked and our answers follow in each section:

Please provide your thoughts or feelings regarding the following:

Any emotional impact this crime may have had on you and those close to you, including changes in relationships, fears, or the need for professional assistance:

We will never be the same as we live a new normal, but we welcome the tears as we miss our son Quinton Stone Jackson. While I underwent extensive psychotherapy, Kristine underwent very little and neither of us anticipates any future "professional assistance." Our daughter on the other hand is struggling significantly. We are unsure if her difficulties are associated with the fact that she turns eighteen years old on May 27 or because she witnessed the accident and lost her brother, but we are worried about her. We hope to keep her from getting into significant trouble and do expect she will need future professional assistance. She has had some psychotherapy to date, but she hasn't committed enough to it to realize any benefit. At this point she thinks she alone is suffering.

Any physical effects of this crime such as injuries and physical pain. You may also want to include details about how long the injuries have lasted, or how long they are expected to last. Describe any medical treatment you have received or expect to receive:

Both Kristine and I will be in physical pain for the rest of our lives. My knees and ankles hurt while Kristine's whole body aches. I had microfracture surgery on my left knee in the year after the accident and am not supposed to run or lift weights, but my injuries pale in comparison to Kristine who had five broken ribs, a broken fibula, a blow to the head, extensive scarring on her back that will require plastic surgery and severe nerve damage throughout her body. Kristine is essentially partially disabled in that she can no longer work a full time desk job due to the pain in her body and can no longer stand the pain of long drives, meaning drives longer than six hours. Kristine requires at the very least monthly massages, weekly chiropractic care and has undergone nerve regeneration therapy with the Centeno-Shultz treatment facility.

Any effect of the crime on the important tasks you normally do:

What is important has been turned upside down. The tasks I once felt important no longer carry the same weight. The reports, budgets, meetings, the job is now secondary. The "crime" has changed the way I live my life. Because I know the essence of Quinton continues to exist, and he has made this known to us, I now have the courage to do things that I *never* would have before. Because of the "crime," I now know I am not in control, nor am I afraid. Now I am an assistant football coach and can directly impact the lives of the young men (who many remind me of Quinton) in a favorable way. I never would have done this before the "crime" took place. Now I am writing a book called *Quinton's Messages*. I never would have done this (*if the "crime" had not occurred*). Now I am president elect for the Denver BOMA chapter (Building Owners and Managers Association) and I never would have had the courage to accept this post. Now I am sharing Quinton's messages of love, compassion, tolerance and of a larger reality; the things I fretted about before are now secondary.

Any comments relating to your financial or property loss (please use the enclosed Declaration of Victim Losses to indicate dollar amounts):

We were fully insured, other than the cost of Quinton's cremation, which will be listed on the above-mentioned declaration.

Any comments about what you would like to see happen to the defendant as a result of the case:

While we have suffered the most unimaginable loss, that loss being our son Quinton Stone Jackson. We do not bear Amanda any ill will. The reason we feel this way is multi-fold. We felt change coming before the accident even took place. The entire family felt unease before this trip. In fact, we changed our usual vacation plans in an effort to avoid death. During the vacation I had a vision that indicated Quinton would be leaving us, not a dream, a vision. And then the accident itself, which was so improbable that we walked away with the understanding that what happened was preordained. Since then, we have continually seen Quinton, heard Quinton. He comes to us in dreams and visions, so we know beyond the shadow of a doubt that he still is. This is a gift that has put our lives on a new path, a new direction that contains a profound knowledge.

What we don't know is why Amanda is part of this tragedy. I put myself in her shoes; I saw her face at the accident scene when she walked up to

Quinton and me. I saw her grief over the scene she was part of. Every parent's worst nightmare is to lose a child. Another equally harrowing nightmare is to be responsible for the death of another human being. Both Kristine's and my nightmare came true and I believe, based upon the expression on Amanda's face at the accident scene, her nightmare came true as well. Here is a young lady, commuting between college and home, while not under the influence of drugs or alcohol. She fell asleep at the exact time and place to be part of this scene. What are the odds?

Just as we were destined to lose Quinton, we believe Amanda was destined to be part of this tragedy. Just as we have learned from this nightmare, we know Amanda is destined to learn from it as well. We wish Amanda well; we wish Amanda a long, productive life filled with love and positive experiences. We wish Amanda is open to and learns whatever she is intended to learn from this awful experience and <u>we **DO NOT BELIEVE** she can best learn this lesson behind bars</u>. Maybe part of her lesson is to know she is forgiven, and by living a productive life she will be honoring our son Quinton Stone Jackson.

Please do not sentence Amanda to any jail time.

___Signature_____   ___Date_____

This document was submitted to the court on April 26, 2011, and became a matter of public record. Ultimately, Amanda, her family, her attorney, the assistant district attorney and the judge saw it. I expect they all saw this document during the month of May, which was important as the court date loomed. Meanwhile, we prepared for our annual vacation and mentally prepared for court.

I was concerned how Kristine and Cheyanne would react to seeing Amanda in person. I was so concerned that I tried to convince them to fly to Phoenix from our home in Conifer so I could attend the court hearing alone and further advocate for leniency. They were just about convinced to let me have my way until our good friend, Chris Voldrich, had an opportunity to weigh in on the matter. Needless to say, Chris was pretty direct and convinced me that we should stand together, united in court. In doing so, we would send a much stronger message, that we were united in our forgiveness.

As the date of the hearing arrived, we loaded up together and drove south. When we pulled into Durango, Colorado on June 2, all three of us were on edge, trying to hold it together. Kristine's stomach was upset, Cheyanne was apprehensive and weepy, and I was trying to hold it together as I focused on breathing while trying to project a calming energy toward Kristine and Cheyanne. Often, in times like these, I find myself focusing my attention on the well-being of others, maybe in an effort to avoid facing my own feelings.

We arrived in Durango about an hour early, as planned, but could not find the courthouse. After calling the victims advocate for directions, we arrived at the court house. The victims advocate and her assistant were actually standing outside waving their arms to get our attention. It was as if the red carpet had been rolled out for us. We parked, 45 minutes early, and were invited to come inside. We declined because we wanted to ground ourselves outside in the sun. As we sat outside, both Kristine and I talked to Cheyanne about breathing deeply to calm her nerves. We sat in silence for 30 minutes in a quasi-meditative state, enjoying the warm, sunny day.

As we sat outside, I saw who I thought were Amanda's family, but I didn't see Amanda. After waiting a few more minutes we made our way in and were greeted again by the victims advocate. We went through the security station and metal detector, then up to the second floor and finally into a small conference room where we met the assistant district attorney. They clearly were focused on us and our well-being--and rightfully so. The tension was tangible. We chatted for a while as they laid out how the proceedings would go.

During this conversation, I asked if I could speak during the proceedings. Using one of my then favorite techniques of self-deprecating humor, I prefaced my request with the statement "not that it (my addressing the court) would make any difference." The assistant district attorney jumped on that statement and let me know that what I had to say would indeed make a difference and in doing so confirmed that I would be allowed to speak. We also asked if we could speak with Amanda directly. The assistant district attorney and victim's advocate looked at each other pensively and then told us they would have to ask Amanda if she wanted to speak with us. Meanwhile, Cheyanne, who feels emotions deeper than both Kristine and I, was really struggling to hold it together. God bless our victim's advocate who began focusing her attention toward Cheyanne, telling her to focus on her breathing during our remaining time in the conference room and as we made our way to the courtroom. During this time Cheyanne said she saw Amanda, but I still didn't recognize her.

We walked into the courtroom and sat down in a row on the left side of the room – me, Kristine and then Cheyanne. Amanda, her attorney, her mom and grandmother sat on the right side of the courtroom, with Amanda and her attorney in the front row. The tension mounted. We stood as Magistrate David L. West came in and then sat down; the proceedings started. During this process I had the sense that people didn't quite know how to take us, maybe not comprehending this demonstration of forgiveness that was about to unfold, or possibly they were expecting us to change our position altogether.

I looked to my right toward Amanda. She was there, but still unrecognizable to me. For two years she carried this burden, the burden of believing she was responsible for the death of another, the death of our son Quinton. From the accident scene, I remembered her being somewhat thin with a clear complexion, but as she sat in the courtroom on June 2, 2011 she looked at least 50 pounds heavier, had severe acne and a significant cough. My heart ached for her; the emotional load she had been carrying was evident to anyone paying attention.

Soon after the proceedings started, I was asked to come up to the podium to have my say. Oddly, as verbose as I can be at times, my comments were brief. Standing in the court I had the sense that I was in a reverent place; respecting the court, judge and attorneys, and that everyone's time was important. I said, "You have our victim's statement, and I am standing here to reiterate our position that we do not want Amanda to serve any jail time. For us, the accident felt preordained, and we were meant to be there in order to learn some significant lessons. While I can't speak for Amanda, we believe that she was part of this tragedy to learn some important lesson as well. We think serving time in jail would only detract from her learning whatever lesson she needs to learn." As I was speaking, I looked at the judge, but when I spoke about life lessons, specifically a lesson for Amanda, I saw her lean forward in her chair and look at me.

At some point not long after I spoke, Amanda's attorney asked if she could address the court. I was surprised, and really didn't know what to expect. I still believe her address to the court was unplanned. Wouldn't you know it; she stood up and shared with the court what her life lesson was from this shared nightmare. She shared that she has a son named Eli and at the time of the accident, he was six-months old. Amanda indicated that she was more focused on her college degree and was neglecting her son. Her lesson, in short, was to stop taking him for granted and be more present in his life. This was a pleasant surprise to us.

Up to this point, the proceedings were going quickly. Weeks ago, Amanda entered a guilty plea, so it was time to go into the sentencing portion of the hearing. This is where the magic occurred, and I had yet another epiphany. The judge spoke for what must have been 15 or 20 minutes. During this time I began to realize just how unusual and how amazing this act of forgiveness truly was. I hadn't really thought of it in those terms during this whole process as our act of forgiveness, our demonstration of forgiveness was only done because it was the right thing for us to do. In the courtroom, I began to realize what they saw playing out before them wasn't something they see very often.

As the judge spoke, he seemed to be in awe of us and seemed to be struggling to understand our perspective. Suddenly, I had the epiphany. Up to this point I had thought our act of forgiveness was an act of free will. The epiphany was realizing our demonstration of forgiveness was just as preordained as the accident itself. As I realized the impact of our actions, not only on Amanda and her family, but the judge and everybody in the courtroom, I understood. They all looked at us in awe, amazement and even reverence.

They truly could not comprehend us, because we were forgiving this young lady who, from society's standards, was responsible for the death of our son. I could see and feel that they were being profoundly impacted by what they were witnessing. And they would share this amazing event with everyone they knew for maybe the rest of their lives. The act of forgiveness is powerful but something that seems rare in our world today. As I thought about this epiphany, I realized, of course, our forgiveness was preordained; our Lord and Savior made us and knew how we would respond in these exact circumstances. Amazing!

As I reflected on this discovery and the implications of it, the judge spent a lot of time explaining why he was going to rule the way he was going to rule – a lot of time. We had been clear, consistent and direct that we wanted Amanda to have no jail time. As the judge spoke he said he was ruling with Amanda's own mental health in mind while taking our expressed wishes into consideration. Finally, he was ready to share his decision and ruled that Amanda serve 10 days. He wanted her to heal; he wanted her to know that she did serve time, in essence paying her debt to society and maybe somehow, to herself. She was to leave immediately after the hearing thereby serving her time in Durango instead of reporting later and going to another location farther away.

As the proceedings ended, we waited patiently while Amanda said her goodbyes to her family. Amanda and her attorney not only agreed to visit with us after the hearing, they were eager to. As she was saying her goodbyes, she looked up and saw us. She walked over to us tentatively with her hand outstretched for me to shake, but I stepped toward her and embraced her. Often, as I remember this moment, I start crying; I spoke in her ear and let her know that we had been worried about her and wished her well. As I stepped away from our embrace, Kristine and Cheyanne came over to hug her as well.

Somewhere in this process, she broke down while trying to tell us something that we just could not make out initially. I asked her to repeat herself. She was telling us about her grandfather, a medicine man who had been deceased for 10 years at the time of the accident. She was asking us how he had appeared. It was at this point she shared that he had been in the car with her after the accident, obviously in spirit. We connected the dots, realizing she had either seen the Vimeo video (www.vimeo.com/7314888) or heard about us speaking of a medicine man who told us that Quinton had made contact. Time was short so we couldn't discuss this in greater detail, but we did exchange contact information. We would subsequently talk, e-mail and visit later during the summer of 2011. Interestingly enough, when Amanda came out of the Durango jail 10 days later, the chronic case of bronchitis she had been battling for months was cured! We believe in part, this is exactly what the judge had in mind.

Much is made of our act of forgiveness. It is important to point out that our forgiveness of Amanda was not an "act" or a "work." We were not forgiving Amanda because we thought we needed to check a box to follow what Jesus said about forgiveness in the New Testament:

- Matthew 6:12 – *"and forgive us our sins as we have forgiven those who sin against us."*
- Matthew 18:35 – *"That's what my heavenly Father will do to you if you refuse to forgive your brothers and sisters from your heart."*
- Luke 6:37 – *"Do not judge others, and you will not be judged. Do not condemn others, or it will all come back against you. Forgive others and you will be forgiven.*

Our act of forgiveness came from the heart. Somehow, it was a spontaneous forgiveness, without understanding the implications. My act of forgiveness came *before* I read the words of Christ above or what other religions say about forgiveness below:

- Islam – *"But if you pardon and exonerate and forgive, Allah is Ever-Forgiving, Most Merciful."* (Qur'an, 64:14)
- Hinduism – *"Forgiveness is, among many things, virtue, sacrifice, truth and holiness. He who truly understands this will be capable of forgiving everything. It is forgiveness that is holding the universe together."* (Interfaith Inspiration for Our Globalized World, 2010)
- Buddhism– *"Never is hate diminished by hatred. It is only diminished by love. This is an eternal law."* (Interfaith Inspiration for Our Globalized World, 2010)
- Jainism–*"I forgive all souls: let all souls forgive me. I am on friendly terms with all. I have no animosity toward anyone."* Jain's Prayer of Forgiveness (Interfaith Inspiration for Our Globalized World, 2010)
- Hare Krishna – *"26 transcendental qualities include Fearlessness – aversion to faultfinding, compassion and freedom from covetousness, gentleness, modesty and steady determination; forgiveness, cleanliness, freedom from envy and the passion for honor!"* Bhagavad-Gita 16.1-3 (Interfaith Inspiration for Our Globalized World, 2010)

Quinton's Legacy

This is a significant part of the magic along our journey. We learned something else remarkable as we visited with Amanda and her family after the hearing. We found out that in 1999 her family was in that very courtroom forgiving a drunk driver who had taken the life of one of their family members. As I took in this information, I remembered that Quinton was born in 1999. What a coincidence! But by then, I'd learned that coincidences often point to a larger picture of our reality and are not coincidences at all. While I don't know the meaning of this particular coincidence, it is clear from subsequent conversations with Amanda that the lives of our families are intertwined.

At this point, we parted ways. Amanda went to jail, and we continued our drive south to Rocky Point for our annual vacation to celebrate our departed loved ones, Quinton and Ed, who passed six years and two days apart. This was indeed a time of healing for all of us. As Kristine stated, it was important for us all to be present, to move forward. In order for one of us to heal, we all needed to heal. From that point on we did.

Chapter Three

WEEKEND ON THE RESERVATION
THE RIPPLE EFFECT OF FORGIVENESS

<u>Quinton's Lesson</u>: *Forgiveness is the gift that keeps giving!*

The rest of the trip down to Rocky Point was uneventful, just like the first half before Amanda's sentencing. For that matter, just like the vacation trip in 2010, the first after Quinton's transition, we didn't feel as if something was chasing us. After our vacation ended, including my fun with the dolphins (discussed in a later chapter), we made the trek home to Colorado. Not long after that, we reached out to Amanda who had served her 10 days. She was now free. Free in more ways than one. Free from jail, free from the chronic case of bronchitis that she had been fighting, and on some level, free of the burden she had been carrying around with her.

At this point in our journey, two years had passed since Quinton had transitioned. During that time I had read numerous New Thought books, the New Testament and a few books about the Native American tribes including: *Dine; Hopi; People of the Red Earth: American Indians of Colorado; The Wisdom of the Native Americans; House of Rain; The Ancient Southwest; Lame Deer Seeker of Visions;* and *The Atlas of the North American Indian.* My interest in reading within this particular genre was a direct result of where Quinton died. This part of the world is special and sacred; the area has been populated for 12,000 years (source: *The Ancient Southwest* by David E. Stuart – University of New Mexico Press 2009). To further illustrate, a co-worker who I didn't know, and had very general information about us, guessed the location of our accident after learning of its odd circumstances. In short, due to the location of the accident, the medicine man and what we had learned up until that point, I was curious to know more.

During conversations with Amanda, I told her that I had an interest in her native culture and would like to learn more. Within a week of our first conversation, Amanda invited us to spend the weekend with her and her family on the Navajo reservation. She let us know that a ceremony was planned for Saturday, August 6, 2011, but didn't provide any more details. I told Kristine that I wanted to go and from there we made the arrangements.

The plan was that I get off work a couple of hours early on Friday. Then we'd drive six hours to Cortez where we could spend the night. We would meet Amanda, her mom and grandmother for breakfast at her home on Saturday morning at 7:00 a.m. Everything went as planned. We made it to Cortez without incident and checked into the Best Western–Turquoise Inn. After a good night of sleep, we rose early and began our drive to Aneth, Utah, a short, 30-minute drive. We still didn't know the full scope of what was in store for us.

We arrived at Amanda's home at the appointed time, and the significance of this trip was not lost upon us. We were going to visit the young lady who played a role in the death of our son. Even though we took a higher point of view, there was no escaping the fact that our initial contact could be not only awkward, but potentially volatile. Both Kristine and I worked to keep our energy soft and non-threatening as we pulled up to their home.

As we stepped up to their side door and saw them making breakfast, it was clear they were feeling the same. The awkwardness passed quickly as we sat down and started talking over the wonderful breakfast they had prepared for us. During the course of the conversation, they told us we had roughly a two-hour drive ahead of us, and the ceremony would last through the night. I was surprised, "What ceremony?"

They explained that we were invited to take part in a sacred Navajo ceremony. This was completely unexpected, but I was game. I wasn't going to miss out on this experience just because I had to be back to work on Monday or wasn't mentally prepared. We finished breakfast quickly as it was time to leave for Lukachakai, Arizona. Because there were six of us going, we took two vehicles, and Amanda quickly volunteered to ride with us.

The one-and-a-half-hour drive passed quickly as we talked about Amanda's family, her school, her upbringing on the reservation and other subjects. A couple of things stood out in my mind. Amanda shared that she had driven past the site where our accident happened her whole life. She remembered while being driven by the site one time at the age of six she thought, "What an awful place to have an accident." It seems like she had a premonition that our paths would cross at that exact location someday. This is yet another example that our reality goes a lot deeper than any of us realize. The other thing that stuck with me was the attitude of her friends about our visit and her response to them. Simply stated, her friends thought she was crazy for meeting with us and asked her if she worried about us being "mean to her." I understand their suspicion of us. Lord only knows what someone would be capable of in this situation. Her response was, "This is what they want." This was amazing, but it was about to get a whole lot more incredible.

When we arrived in Lukachakai, which is within the Colorado Plateau, also known as the Painted Desert, we met a group of about 15 or 20 people. At some point we sat down for lunch, and we each introduced ourselves. What a remarkable group! The famous author Luis Rodriguez and his wife Trini sat across from me; and next to them, Hector Herrera and his wife Elisa, and Enrique—all from the Los Angeles area. Trini's nephew Cristian sat on the end along with Enrique's son Jose. Dr. Anthony Lee and his wife Dolores who live in Lukachakai lead the ceremony. Many of their family members sat near Amanda and her family. Nobody knew who we were or why we had joined them. When it was our turn to speak, Cindy, Amanda's mother, introduced us by sharing the tragedy that brought us together. Dr. Lee met Amanda and her mom years prior, and subsequently welcomed them into his spiritual family. Tears were shed as the group listened to the details of that fateful day and everything that had happened since. When we told how hard we worked on Amanda's behalf, they seemed to be in awe of our forgiveness. Proof of the hearing was demonstrated by the fact that we were there together being introduced by Amanda. What an introduction into their lives! The discussion of our demonstration of forgiveness has made us lifelong friends and now *we* are part of their spiritual family.

In no time at all, Kristine rode back to Aneth with Amanda and her family to prepare food for the next day's morning meal. I stayed and helped construct the teepee for the ceremony. It was a hot and dusty August day. Dr. Lee was still recovering from heart surgery a year prior and it was to be his first ceremony since the surgery. None of us, except Dr. Lee and his assistant, had ever constructed a teepee before, and it was more far more complicated than I expected. The process was detailed and exact, with the longest post positioned over the opening; the longest pole had an eagle feather on it. The poles fit into two flaps in order to control the flow of air in and out of the teepee. With their direction, it came together nicely and it was quite impressive.

Next we needed to gather certain vegetation for the ceremony, so we climbed into two vehicles and went on a short drive. Within 15 minutes, we found ourselves in the pine trees with the cool temperatures of the Lukachakai Mountains. The pine trees were easily 100 years old and massive in height and girth. It was totally gratifying to leave the oppressive heat for this refreshing cool air and pine trees in just a few minutes. With the highest point of 9,466 feet above sea level, the beauty of the entire area was awe-inspiring. The area reminded me of Conifer, Colorado or Flagstaff, Arizona. We collected what we needed while enjoying the coolness and camaraderie as we learned more about each other. Pictures were taken and then we headed back to the site of the ceremony for one more important task before the stage was set.

The vegetation was spread around the inside of the teepee along the edges. Come to find out, we would be sitting on it. A five-gallon bucket of what appeared to be beach sand was onsite along with buckets of water. Dr. Lee explained that we were to make a crescent moon with the sand in the middle of the teepee, with the opening of the crescent moon facing the entrance. He explained that the ceremony coincided with the crescent moon outside. We started building the crescent moon inside the teepee and it would grow to eight feet across.

He explained that the beginning of the sand moon starts low and narrow, coinciding with our birth. As the construction of the sand crescent moon continues, it becomes wider and higher, reaching a point where it is approximately six inches high and six inches wide at its midpoint. Dr. Lee told us that midpoint coincides with the midpoint in our own lives; from that point the moon is narrower and lower until it reaches the end of the crescent, coinciding with our death. The symbolism was profound, but not as profound as what he said next. "What is visible is half a moon; the other half is invisible. This represents your time on the other side."

I was blown away; this matched exactly to what I believed to be true; and with what Brian Weiss M.D. and Michael Newton Ph.D. said in their books. It paralleled my knowledge that Quinton is an old soul— he'd been here before. The moon inside the teepee represented the repeating cycle of life.

The teepee was completed. We headed back to Dr. Lee's house for an afternoon where there was a birthday party for one of his grandchildren followed by dinner before the ceremony. I stayed out of the way, as I didn't know anybody well enough to feel comfortable hanging with them. As I circled the house looking for shade, I saw children playing, running, jumping and giggling. One of the children, a girl maybe the age of eight, grabbed my hand beaconing me to follow her. We climbed up and down a mound of dirt. She took me around back to a small stove and we pretended to cook, and then to a small play house where I slid in from the bottom. I was astounded by her precociousness and trust of a total stranger; it was as if she saw the real me, not the burly bald man I had become. Maybe she sensed Quinton around me. In any case, the bond was quick and strong. After a time, I pulled back again, encouraging her to play with the other children, not wanting to seem inappropriate to the adults.

As the sun began to sink, I found myself sitting on the west side of the house watching the shadows of the Lukachakai Mountains elongate. The area is truly beautiful. Serenity overtook me as I sat alone and took it all in. Part of this was an attempt to mentally prepare for the ceremony that would start when the sun went down. As the sun continued to sink toward the horizon, I gathered a plate of food from the table and resumed my post in a chair next to the cooler of water and sodas. My new-found family from L.A. soon joined me, one at a time. We slipped into a conversation about metaphysics, and I suddenly had a powerful sense of déjà vu – that Hector, Enrique, Christian, Jose and I had been here before having this same conversation. As the conversation continued, I remember that this was the first time I had met them, yet it was so familiar. Remarkable!

The time was nearing for the ceremony. While some napped, others cleaned up, and we prepared for a long night. I watched the others, taking cues from them since I really didn't know what to expect, all the while focusing on being centered, grounded and accepting of what was to come. Just before sunset, I drove to the teepee in Q's truck and waited for the rest of the group. Kristine, Amanda and her family hadn't arrived yet, and I began to wonder if they would. But I continued to relax and further calm myself. I was preparing myself to sit in a teepee all night long; just one more part of this crazy journey we had been on since Quinton's transition from this realm. Thankfully, we continue to be willing to explore new ideas. I say we because Kristine continues to be by my side every step of the way—and this night was no different.

Just before it was time for us to step into the teepee, Kristine, Amanda's mom and grandmother arrived. Later, Kristine said, "It was like I spent the day with my family!" That was how comfortable they were together. How does this feeling of comfort happen? Could this be an indication that we knew each other from previous lives; that our lives "crash" into one another in this life and we know each other so profoundly? No matter the reason, this amazing journey of a lifetime continues.

Kristine surprised me by deciding to be in the teepee by my side. At this point I should cease being surprised. Even though she continues to be in pain from the accident (as do I to a much lesser extent) she insisted on sharing this experience with me. Thinking of her comfort, Amanda's mom provided Kristine with a low chair and a beautiful woven blanket – then in we went. As I tried to make myself comfortable on the ground, I looked at Kristine and Enrique with a bit of envy because they got to sit on stadium chairs. He also had back problems.

At some point during the night, Dr. Lee became concerned by something and wanted to go out into the night. He asked me to go with him. He felt the presence of an evil spirit and wanted to ward it off with prayer; he wanted me by his side since I was the largest man there, and probably because I didn't have the sense to be afraid. As we walked out, we stopped by each point on the compass to pray out loud while I stood by him watching attentively. After finishing and feeling satisfied that the evil spirit had left, we went back inside.

By two in the morning my body was in serious pain, while Kristine was in even worse pain. I turned to her and said, "Let's go." I was disappointed. We gave it a whirl but I didn't feel like I got anything from it at all. We stepped out of the teepee and climbed into the truck. Kristine laid down in the back of the cab where she could stretch out, while I ate a sandwich in the driver's seat, then reclined in an effort to get some sleep. Kristine fell asleep immediately. For about 10 minutes or so I fidgeted; sleep would not come. Then I heard a soft knock on my window.

It was Hector; he told me Dr. Lee wanted me back in the ceremony. The old me would have been pretty annoyed and probably declined, but the new me rationalized that it must be important if he wanted me back so much that he sent Hector to collect me. I went back in and sat in Kristine's chair, not knowing what to expect.

Quinton's Legacy

As dawn approached, I had what can be called a mystical experience. While I am not sure what I expected, I didn't expect this. In my mind's eye, I clearly saw Quinton and my father-in-law Ed Cano together laughing at me; I mean they were laughing hysterically at me, but with love! I knew what they were saying! "Look at what you are doing and where you are. Mr. Straight-and-Narrow, you are in a teepee having an experience way off the beaten path of your life."

Suddenly my grandmother Dorothy Jackson was there smiling and then our deceased family friend, Jack Childs. All of them deceased, and all of them in my mind's eye smiling at me in LOVE. Then someone else joined them; it was my father, and my tears started to flow. As I will share later, my dad had shown up in the reading with Cherry Creek, Colorado medium Rebecca Rosen. I had been ashamed at how I felt and what I thought. Where was my forgiveness of my own father, I wondered? Well, as he joined the four of them to make five in my mind's eye, I began crying because he was not only included with them but was also included with them in LOVE! I began to cry because in that moment, I had forgiven him and we had reconciled. And in that moment, I believe the forgiveness freed him – and me as well.

I had been walking around with a chip on my shoulder for a lifetime. Even seven years after my dad's death, I carried this disease with me, which also means dis-ease. I was angry for all the abuse he had heaped on my mom and the fear that was a part of our lives. I thought I had come to terms with it only to discover four months earlier not only had I not come to terms with it, but this dis-ease in my soul had grown. Finally, I was free of it; the burden had been removed. I was free. Now I could think of my father and not feel myself become sad or angry or vengeful. Now I could forgive my father for his shortcomings completely and not let them weigh me down. This is the ripple effect of forgiveness! Once you start from your heart, and not your mind, you really don't know where it may lead. I forgave Amanda. And because I did, I ended up not only forgiving my father but reconciling with him as well. I felt lighter.

And so it is with forgiveness. How many of us will hold on to a pain or a grudge, indefinitely? Why do so many of us do so? Maybe for some of us this is all we have, or all we think we have, but when the pain is released, when we finally reach the place of forgiveness in our heart, we are set free. This is what I experienced in finally letting go of the ill-will I carried toward my father. Forgiveness is a gift for the one forgiving.

Chapter Four

CHRISTMAS AT THE PENDLETONS – 2009

Quinton's Lesson: Angels take on many forms!

We continue to learn so much, just by slowing down and taking time. Trust me, I know just how difficult that is; in a way it is almost easier to get lost in the busyness of life and, in essence, stay blind to the largeness of our reality. On the other hand, how boring is that? Quinton slowed me down to the point where, at times, I was able to have the most amazing experiences. What I relate below speaks to yet another one of those experiences.

The Pendletons have been angels in the flesh for our family. First there was Les; I met him in 1977 when I was 12 years old after my dad moved the family from New Jersey to Colorado. While I am not sure of the specifics of how my Dad and Les met, I do know that it was through the two retail shops my parents owned in downtown Evergreen.

While in my early teens, I remember Les for two things: gathering fire wood for the cold Conifer winters and playing football. As an athlete who played football and baseball, Les had come through the Jefferson County school system about 11 years prior to me. We played catch with the football often, and over time he taught me how to punt and even long snap. Because of his tutelage, I ended up punting for the junior high football team in addition to playing quarterback and defensive back. Les has always been a good guy. He married Cheryl and they had one daughter, Stacey. While it seemed I saw him less as I moved on to high school, they saw me. They, like so many of those close to me, remembered more of my childhood and teen years than I did.

As I shared in *Quinton's Messages*, after high school, I was finally able to leave the nest after earning an athletic scholarship to play football at the University of Wyoming, and subsequently didn't come back to Conifer much at all after 1985. I guess I wanted to put the past behind me, but I will always regret not staying in contact with those who helped me along the way. Fortunately the universe was kind enough to bring so many of them back into my life. Like so many young folks who leave a small town only to yearn for it later, so did I.

Not long after moving back to Conifer in 1998, and probably before Quinton was born, Kristine and I were driving down Highway 285 in Aspen Park. I hadn't seen Les in about 15 years, but as we drove behind a small Pontiac I turned to Kristine excitedly and said, "That looks like Les Pendleton!" How could I possibly recognize anyone from the back of his head? Well, Les is a big man from his years of playing football and lumberjacking, his neck and head merge into his shoulders. While I thought it was Les, I wasn't sure. Still, it had been so many years, and I missed his friendship. I was not going to pass up this opportunity. I did something very risky for anyone living in Colorado. We followed the Pontiac north through Meyers Ranch and up toward Windy Point, but before we made it there the vehicle turned off into Pendleton Ranch.

Now, I was sure it was Les, but a lot of time had passed since he had seen me. Before, I was a boy of 18, but now I was a man and looking a lot different. I began to worry that he would not recognize me. At this point he saw us following him up his parent's driveway, watching us closely in his rear view mirror. He parked and I parked right behind him, jumping out and announcing myself quickly, "Les, it's me, Ernie!" His anxiety passed, he smiled and we embraced. Then he stood back looking at me and repeating "Ernie Jackson, I can't believe it is you, after all these years."

We have stayed in contact ever since. For the next 14 years, we would get together at least once a year at Christmas, have dinner, catch up and exchange presents. We usually met at their home for Christmas, and they came to our home during other visits. We spent a lot of time talking about my dad and my childhood, and how we first came into contact again after all those years.

On more than one occasion they shared memories of me coming by with both of my sisters in my 1968 Camaro; they even said I usually had both of them in the car. This is one of the memories I must have blocked out, along with the more unpleasant memories from my youth. I remembered trying to protect Regina, my youngest sister, by taking her away from the house when my father was on the warpath, but I hadn't remembered taking my middle sister Tina. I wish I knew why my memory is so spotty; maybe I am still learning to be "present." However, I am *more than grateful* for losing many of the painful memories, because those I do recall filled me with rage years later. But I wish I hadn't lost so many good memories in the process.

What was special about Les is also true (if not even more so) of his wife Cheryl and daughter Stacey. They are "present" all the time. Their gifts to us over the years have been meaningful in ways that I can't adequately explain. During their travels and trips, no matter the time of the year or where they were, they'd find the perfect gifts for us and save them until Christmas. Our time together was always special. Even though we were friends living within eight miles of each other, we both were consumed by our jobs, which is why we didn't get together more often. I guess it's the norm for many of us to give too much to our jobs and less time to our loved ones.

The Pendletons had an exceptional bond with Quinton. It was like they knew him on an even deeper level than most others. Part of which may be the fact that they are present, but maybe it is more than that. After what I experienced with them during the first Christmas after Quinton passed, their connection makes more sense. We had always openly referred to them as our angels when we were a family of four, here in the physical world, but even more so after Quinton's transition. There was something special about how they watched over us.

At Quinton's service, Cheryl watched over me without me even knowing it. Only nine days had passed; we were still in a fog from the accident that took our son's life and left Kristine and me badly injured. I stood and spoke with everyone who came to offer their condolences. Noticing I was becoming pale, Cheryl brought me water and asked me to sit down. I accepted the water but remained standing. I felt her watchful eyes, making sure she was close, ready to come to my aid if I wobbled.

As that first painful Christmas without Quinton approached, Cheyanne and Kristine were in Phoenix with my mother-in-law Nellie Cano. Shortly after Quinton's death, Cheyanne was desperate for a change of scenery so they were in Phoenix looking for a home for Cheyanne, Nellie and our young nephew, Alexander Ochoa, to share. I worked in Denver but was preparing to leave the job I had when Quinton passed. Knowing the girls were out of town, Les invited me over for dinner. My evening with them is one that I will never forget.

I showed up and immediately noticed how good Les looked, and told him so. There was something vibrant about him and somehow he looked *younger*. I wasn't sure what it was. His sideburns were different too, not that Les had long sideburns. As I looked at him during the evening meal, the sideburns were cut at an angle like Captain Kirk would wear his in the original Star Trek series. I was present and taking it in and then strange things began to happen.

After dinner Les and I went to the TV room while Cheryl and Stacey cleaned the kitchen and prepared our desserts. As I looked in the kitchen, Cheryl's back was to me, but I could not take my eyes off of her. It looked like a sunbeam was shining on her, or she had a golden aura around her. Cheryl's hair caught my attention; it was somehow, glowing! I was trying not to openly stare into the kitchen, while talking to Les who was on my left, but it was becoming increasingly difficult. When Cheryl and Stacey came into the TV room with strawberry shortcake, Cheryl sat directly in front of me, slightly to my right and Stacey to my right on the same couch beside me. Les and I were still in a conversation, but my mind kept returning to how I perceived Cheryl; I cut my eyes over to her trying not to get caught openly staring at her, in an effort to see if she still looked the same.

Naturally she caught me and, while looking at me straight in my eyes, her expression seemed to say *I know you see us. The real us!* It was as if she had sent me a telepathic message. What a crazy, magical moment and evening. I was beside myself trying to make sense of how I perceived both Les and Cheryl. I saw their true essence; this is the only way I can explain it. And how I saw them defied the age of their earthly bodies. They were different in some way. This so impacted me that I include it here. How often do we dismiss these occurrences, brushing them off as oddities or just as something weird, only to forget and get back to being busy?

As I continued reading about spiritual matters, this experience of seeing our friends in their true form began to make more sense. For instance, when I read Todd Burpo's book, *Heaven is for Real,* about his then five-year-old son (Colton) who had had a near death experience, I thought of this night with the Pendletons. Colton reported going to Heaven, meeting Jesus and his deceased grandfather. The three-year-old explained, "Dad, nobody's old in Heaven, and nobody wears glasses." While Colton, who never met his grandfather in the flesh, could not recognize him in a picture taken when he was 80 years old, recognized him right away when shown a picture of him at 29 years of age (Burpo, Todd, *Heaven is for Real,* Nashville, Tennessee, Thomas Nelson Inc., 2010).

This coincides exactly with what Sylvia Browne writes in her book *Life on the Other Side,* "No matter what age we are when we die, we're all thirty years old on The Other Side" (Browne, Sylvia, *Life on the Other Side,* New York, New York, Penguin Putman, Inc., July 2001). From my perspective, this quote from the Bible validates young Colton and Sylvia, "While we live in these earthly bodies, we groan and sigh, but not that we want to die and get rid of these bodies that clothe us. Rather we want to put on our new bodies so that these dying bodies will be swallowed up by life" (Corinthians 5:4, New Living Translation Second Edition, 2 Tyndale House Publishers, Inc. Carol Stream, Illinois). While the first two references focus on age as a determining factor, I think it has less to do with age and more to do with seeing their souls in a truer form, or maybe seeing their souls peeking through their physical bodies.

A week later we had dinner again. This time Kristine and Cheyanne were back in town. I told Kristine about my prior experience and was eager to see if my perception of them was the same. During the evening I turned to Kristine, telling her they looked "normal" like they always did, even Les' sideburns were back to the same block style. At that point, I even shared with Les, Cheryl and Stacey. We had a good laugh, and Stacey even wondered out loud why I hadn't perceived her differently. I just don't know. All I could do is report that I had perceived them differently the week prior. Perhaps I had been given the gift of seeing them as they appear in spirit.

Chapter Five

SEEING AN AURA

Quinton's Lesson: Pay attention, you might be surprised at what you sense!

Six months had passed since Quinton's transition into what I believe is pure energy, and we had already been immersed into a new journey. I tried going back to work twice at this point, but my heart just wasn't in it. So I permanently resigned from Schnitzer West as of December 31, 2009. Everything was changing quickly, but we were game for learning more – no matter how far outside of the same old box it seemed. What I mean is, we were in uncharted territory; no more of the same daily routine or same perspective on life.

One of the opportunities that came our way was to take part in a past life clairvoyant reading, courtesy of a regression class being taught by Mia Foley, not far from our home in Conifer. We're not sure if Kristine found Mia Foley's flyer in the mail or if we were invited by one of the three sisters, Linda Levine, Melody Conaghan, or Debra Hundemer, who had attended Mia's courses previously. In any case, we were game for the experience not only to find out who we were in previous lives, but also we were curious about the course and what we may experience by participating.

The three of us showed up at the appointed time – Kristine, Cheyanne and me. We were bundled up because the weather was cold and snowy. We pulled up to the Marshdale office building, parked and went inside shaking off the cold and snow. The class was upstairs. We found places to sit in the room. As we looked around, we noticed several women taking part in the class, and we were pleasantly surprised to see our neighbor, Kris Otto. Debra Hundemer was there, too. We had known Debra before but got to know her even better after the accident. She had performed Reiki on us in an effort to help us with our aches and pains. Seeing so many familiar faces among the students who would be performing the readings helped us to relax even further.

Once everyone was assembled, Mia divided us into groups and assigned her students among the three of us. Kristine and Cheyanne each had five students assigned to them, and I had three. As we were directed to our respective rooms, I met a woman in the hallway who almost seemed to be glowing – she was very upbeat, positive, happy and excited. I was pleased that she was part of the three who were going to work with me. Her name was Heidi Saltzman.

When we got into the room, we sat down with them on one side of the table and me on the other. It felt kind of odd sitting that way, as opponents or adversaries often sit this way. But I didn't give it another thought. We chatted briefly as we settled in; and as the time neared for them to start, they began to meditate quietly with their eyes closed. I closed my eyes too, even though they told me not to. Subsequently, I had one of the most astounding experiences in my life!

As I sat there looking forward with my eyes closed, I realized that I was seeing an image. The image was black, a silhouette in the shape of a head, hair and shoulders. I had been looking at it for some time without understanding what I was seeing. Once I realized what it was, I opened my eyes. Heidi, the woman with the amazing energy, the one who was now sitting in front of me, was who I saw with my eyes closed. I opened my eyes and knew it was a perfect match. I was totally present but doubting myself. Because the room was dimly lit, I knew the image I saw with my eyes closed could not have been the result of a bright light behind Heidi.

I closed my eyes again and the silhouette was still there; it seemed as if I was seeing the energy from around her. I slowly kept opening and closing my eyes. It was her all right, but then I wondered if I could see the other women that same way. Keeping my eyes closed, slowly I turned my head slightly to the right, where the woman in the middle sat, to see if I could see her image. I opened my eyes and repeated the process with the other women. They were there, but when I closed my eyes to look, I could not see either the same way I saw Heidi. Still, I wondered if somehow I was imagining this as I turned back to Heidi and repeated the procedure. I could still see her shape through my closed eyes. *Wow,* I thought in total amazement! I saw energy radiate from her, which was her aura.

An aura is our individual energy or, maybe better put, the soul that others can sense beyond our bodies. For many of those gifted to see them, they see them in the form of a color. These colors represent some attribute of the person it is emanating from. For instance, a yellow-green aura is said to represent being a good communicator, and a pale yellow aura is said to represent recently embarking on a spiritual journey or having recently discovered some latent psychic ability.

Then it was time for the reading, but nothing could compare to this experience that completely amazed me. They did a rose reading. Heidi explained that to find a past life, they look on the stem of a rose to see how far back the life was; the farther down the stem, the older the lifetime. By now, as you can imagine, my eyes were wide open as I listened intently to what they were telling me. While they called it a rose reading, they said mine was like a lotus flower in that it was open and ready to learn. They also said that I had a long and rigid stem signifying I have been here before, numerous times. The message about being open and ready to learn resonated with me; Quinton had set the stage for that with his early departure and subsequent visits.

Having many past lives was harder to connect with. While I understand and believe this to be true, I can't help but wonder why

I continue to struggle with issues around expressing my emotions, reliance on food, and mindless busyness as my emotional crutches. Maybe in another life I starved or something. Well, why should I be any different than others? It takes time, lifetimes in fact, to overcome some deep-seated issues.

Next, they shared what they had picked up as my past lives, which were quite profound as I definitely connect with both lives within my current lifetime. They first shared that I was a "head monk" somewhere. They did not mention a religion or geography, but something inside of me thinks that this may be where I picked up my affinity for trees, nature and mountains. Through much of my current lifetime I longed to be in the mountains and, no matter where I am, I always plant trees that will grow large to provide shade and ambience. They continued by saying I was happy in that role. Priests were around me, looking to me for guidance, direction and wisdom. They said I had an easy and happy life. They shared that my transition was peaceful, and that I was surrounded by my disciples within the monastery. I found the description of this lifetime very interesting, as I find myself in this mode often. I consciously and unconsciously help others, lift them up and assist them in understanding the meaning of their own purpose in life. I am blessed that this is not a coincidence at all.

They continued, "Half way down the stem is usually gold, but yours is diamonds, probably representing royalty." When they opened the ring they saw a picture of a Viking. They saw me on a Viking ship with big sails, cold winds and a fur coat. They described me in that lifetime as powerful and respected but not the captain. They went on to say I had a lot of power but not a lot of responsibility. I struggled to scribble down the notes, as they continued by saying I was very serious, and people feared me. Apparently I liked this image during that lifetime; they said I was lonely as I focused on maintaining this image. I find it interesting that my birth name in my current lifetime, Ernest, is often misspelled as Earnest. As you probably know, being earnest is defined in numerous places as being serious. What is even more interesting is that much of my early life was spent just this way – I was serious and rarely smiled. Did that lifetime as a Viking also leak into my current life? It certainly seems possible, as I experience elements of both those past lifetimes within my current incarnation as Ernie Jackson.

We finished by discussing layers of the Aura, which consisted of seven layers of my struggles. Within my struggles lie my greatest opportunities for improvement. And if I have the courage to face them, I can rise to a new level of spiritual evolution.

The session ended and the three of us went home, but seeing Heidi's true essence, her energy, her aura–through closed eyes–stuck with me. I wanted to tell her about this experience, but didn't. Months later, I literally bumped into her and took the opportunity to share what I saw. When she said, "I felt it, too," I was rocked onto my heels. I know I am still a relatively young soul because this was just too much for me to digest – too much for me to comprehend. I literally ran away. The experience of a metaphysical connection can be wondrous, unusual and difficult to comprehend, all at the same time. My wish for myself is to not turn and run the next time I am confronted with a situation that is beyond my current comprehension.

Since this event, the three of us have been blessed to get to know Heidi better. Heidi clarified the difference between a past life regression, where the subject's eyes are closed and taken into a trance to re-live the experience, and a prior life while during a clairvoyant reading, when you don't have to close your eyes.

Heidi is definitely an old soul here to help the world; she is definitely a very bright light!

Chapter Six

LEARNING AND MY GUARDIAN ANGEL

Quinton's Lesson: God loves each and every one of us!

The traditional grief counseling and then traditional psychotherapy I experienced for the months after Quinton transitioned was a Godsend. My doctor's office was near downtown Denver on Grant Street, and his name was Dan. He is good at his craft, and I felt I had a strong connection with him. So much so that I brought Kristine, Cheyanne and Cheyanne's best friend Layla in for a session. But logistically it wasn't feasible for them to see him regularly, as they were in the Conifer area, which was about a 35-minute drive.

Dan and I worked together for the better part of a year as we tried collectively to get my arms around our tragedy and begin to get me in touch with my emotions. Losing a child is every parent's worst nightmare, but I continued to be emotionally detached. I remember Dan asking if I was mad at God. The question totally perplexed me, although I understand it better now based upon what I have read about grieving.

After a loss, many people are mad at God, as pointed out in *A Grief Observed* by C.C. Lewis, (Harper One, March 3, 2009). Some even lose their faith for an extended period of time, if not permanently. Me, on the other hand, I felt like I found God through the accident! And what a dichotomy that is; I often describe it as a divine and awful dichotomy as we live with the "loss" of our child while at the same time discover that our son hasn't really died at all.

When I give a presentation or share our journey informally with others who have suffered a loss, I feel strongly that we are not to compare or contrast each other's experiences. Death is death. It is a tough experience in western civilization because the common consensus is that death is forever and might even be contagious in some way. When I share, sometimes people shake their heads telling me, "I have lost a parent (or sibling), but my loss can't compare to losing a child." Sure it can. The transition of a loved one is a transition; it is awful and painful, often leaving a giant hole in our hearts that may never be filled. Don't disparage your experience by comparing it to someone else's experience.

While I say this, I am ashamed to say that the way in which I relate to our accident – actually finding God through it – must cause pain for some, but this is my experience. Maybe I need to do a better job of explaining my discovery in a more sensitive way. In saying, "I found God" on that fateful day, I am acknowledging the fact that Quinton left us in a merciful way; he did not suffer. He was here in the physical world one second and the next he was gone. That accident could have been so much worse, and if it had, I just don't know how I would have coped. In any of those worst-case scenarios that we were spared, I imagine I may have been mad at God; and if I were, my emotions would have been even more amplified. But that isn't what happened. Quinton was here one second and gone the next while we, after being hit by a bouncing airborne car, are still here walking around seemingly in perfect health.

For months I saw Dr. Dan on a weekly basis, sharing my spiritual journey of enlightenment. He was right about one thing. I was angry and had been angry for much of my life. I became so good at swallowing my anger, almost nobody knew about it until it bubbled to the surface with a force that surprised even me.

Quinton's Legacy

Once, during a meeting at Cherry Creek, I suddenly snapped, becoming confrontational regarding an issue relating to the future development of the area I no longer remember. What I do remember is being surprised and ashamed after the white-hot anger dissipated. It bothered me and frightened me. I apologized to the gentleman who was the recipient of my anger, as well as the others who attended the meeting. Thankfully they understood, knowing my personal situation and joked, "Was that the best you could do?" But I knew how monstrous that anger felt in my heart; I thought I had my anger under control.

As Dan and I discussed that episode, we went all the way back to my childhood, living in fear of my dad, his outbursts, his beatings and verbal abuse of my mom over the years. We talked about my feelings of helplessness to do anything to resolve it. This is where the anger began. He told me that I had to get to know my anger, to which I shook my head. "There is no way. My anger scares the hell out of me." At its worst, it seems I can barely hold it back, with the key phrase being *it seems*. If it truly was as bad as I made it seem, I would be in jail or dead by now.

During the last months of working with Dr. Dan, we tried to get to know my anger and find a voice for a wide range of emotions that I had been suppressing. We never reached it to his satisfaction or mine. I just can't, I still tend to hold back part of myself, not giving it all up – even to this day. On more than one occasion, I sighed deeply before responding to a question, and he'd pounce, "What was that?" And when I didn't understand, he'd say, "That sigh – what was that?" I honestly didn't know at the time and would tell him so. Even today, the "sigh" is still with me and within it, my emotions – the sadness, the resignation, the regret, the disappointment. The list goes on.

During one of the last sessions with him, I explained that through the violence, fear and warped coping mechanisms of my father – of my mom's victimhood – I was amazed that the impact was not as great as it could have been. My feeling was that I was being protected by something external; something that placed a bubble around me that insulated me from the horror. I went into great detail explaining how that thing, external to myself, protects me to this day in other ways. He did not understand. In a gentle way, he told me it was my imagination and whatever I felt protecting me came from within. Shortly after that, I knew our work was complete. He'd given me much, but I needed more. I knew, I always knew, that something external watched over and protected me in some way. I just didn't have a name for it.

I started a life-shaping course facilitated by Leianne Wilson during the final two months or so of psychotherapy. Life shaping resonated with me; I knew this was the next step of my journey. During one of the first sessions of the course, we were given an L-shaped piece of a metal hanger with one end in a piece of cut-off straw. While holding the end held by the straw and using my mind, I learned that I could make the L shaped piece of metal rotate. It was a pretty cool way to start the course. It was later that I noticed that my hand, holding the end of the straw, sometimes moved as I tried to get the metal to rotate by using my mind. Ah, the skeptic rears his head and that is okay. Being skeptical is healthy. We need to question everything as we journey down the rabbit hole. But the point remains: we can manifest so much by the power of our mind; by having faith. Even the Bible tells us, "Because you believed, it has happened" (Matthew 8:13 NLT).

It was during this course that I discovered more about how I conducted myself; it blew my mind! While I appeared to have survived a painful childhood, I was deeply afraid. At some point during my life, my ego developed a rather amazing coping mechanism. As Leianne took me through her course, she explained how our ego's primary function is, simply put, to ensure that we are okay and that we feel okay (Wilson, Leianne, *Life Shaping Questions: Your Bridge to Shaping the Life you Desire!*, Charleston, SC, August 2, 2012). After the kind of childhood I'd experienced, how could I be okay? As a teenager, I became an over-achiever and people pleaser. As I grew into manhood, then to middle age, this coping mechanism was out of control, and this is where I completely lost myself.

Day after day, week after week, year after year, I rarely gave myself a break. I was feverishly trying to comfort myself – to feel okay. Yes, I worked hard to make money and provide for my family, but unknown to me, my job served another function. It made me feel good about myself – made me feel okay. Sadly, for much of my life, the fear of failure was the overriding motivator. Perceiving myself as failing at something would destroy my self-image. Reflecting on my life, at times I would avoid failing by quitting. I am pretty sure this is rationale I use for not dancing. I don't know how, and I imagine I'd look silly practicing, so why bother. I wonder how many things I've missed out on because of this warped thinking.

Taking this mania to an extreme, when home on the weekends in the most beautiful place amongst the pine trees and wildlife, I continued to work. Still trying to be okay. I was like the energizer bunny- painting, washing cars and windows, cutting down dead trees, and chopping wood to the point of exhaustion. I rarely gave myself a break and rarely just sat quietly in appreciation of it all–my family, the beauty of the area– all that I should have been appreciating. I pushed myself to the breaking point, and when I was finally ready to break the cycle, Quinton's time on earth was almost over. I was ready to listen, to learn, to ask for help.

I suspect that this state of mind, this readiness to deal with the unknown issue that I hadn't faced in a previous lifetime, may be part of the master plan. As told in *Quinton's Messages,* I learned that Quinton and I had "done this before," but I didn't learn my lesson; therefore, we elected to do it again. Now, four years later, I see the synchronicity of finally being ready to change, even asking for help to change. By leaving the physical world, Quinton assisted me. Going deeper still, I understand a truer purpose of adversity, adversity of any kind. Adversity is an opportunity to learn and grow. I make that statement as a result of what we have been through and just how much I have grown from it.

So there I was in Leianne Wilson's life-shaping course. The key for me, the most important hurdle, was to break the cycle of an overactive ego. My goal was to finally realize that I was okay. Simple, right? For some, maybe, but for me it is one of the toughest struggles. My own self-doubts got in my way of finding this peaceful place, not to mention the imagined doubts others may have about me. It's a constant struggle to realize that I am okay; to know it, believe it and then live it! Even after achieving this lofty perch, I must be diligent against falling from it tomorrow. And when I inevitably do, pick myself back up, forgive myself and seek it again.

The struggle continues in my head with a voice that doubts me, or loses faith in me in some way. This voice in my head, my ego, tells me I must do something, anything to feel worthy. And I must not fail. This is the value of meditation. If our ego allows us the time; sitting quietly for any period of time thinking about nothing but knowing we are okay, we are loved. Love can get us back to being centered and put the ego in its place. And so many of us fight the same battle; I really think those of us fighting this fight are in the majority, and those old souls comfortable in their own skin are the minority.

This thought coincides with what Michael Newton, Ph.D., wrote in his book, *Journey of Souls*, "I believe almost three quarters of all souls who inhabit human bodies on Earth today are still in the early stages of development. I know this is a grossly discouraging statement because it means most of our human population is operating at the lower end of their training. On the other hand, when I consider a world population beset by so much negative cross-cultural misunderstanding and violence, I am not inclined to change my opinion about the high percentage of lower level souls on Earth." I agree with Dr. Newton relating to the point of being okay, and why so many of us seem to thrash about in our lives.

As I delved deeper into the course, we addressed the conversations going on in my mind; here I learned that I am no different than anyone else. My mind seems to run a million miles per hour. It seemed like I was living in my head more than I lived in the world; often when surprised by an unexpected event, I wasn't present enough to react naturally and would lock up. To prevent this from happening again, I'd go over myriads of imagined events in an effort to figure out how to respond. This is no way to live!

During the course I learned that most of my thoughts or inner conversations that seemed original, innovative or profound were merely automatic responses based upon the associations I had developed during my life. To make matters worse, my associations were, in most cases, false. Here is an example. Previously, I associated adversity with something I wanted to desperately avoid, but I have since learned that this is a false association. I now associate adversity with an opportunity to learn something I may have not already learned; it is an opportunity for growth, for spiritual growth at that.

My acceptance that *I am okay* was even more impactful to my life than the traditional psychotherapy. We have all been through a myriad of hurts, disappointments and putdowns through our lives. If we can simply understand that it wasn't our fault, and it had absolutely nothing to do with us, we could save ourselves a lifetime of *trying to be okay*. We must learn to forgive ourselves for the hurts that we have inflicted on others while asking forgiveness of those we have hurt. In many ways, asking for the forgiveness of others is easier than forgiving ourselves. While that is another topic, it is a hard truth that I am still battling with the ego, one that does not tolerate my mistakes.

My Guardian Angel

As my time with Leianne came to a close, another mystical experience surprised me. I had experienced many, courtesy of Quinton, but for some reason I not only stopped seeking them out, I avoided them. I thought that the chapter of my life of having mystical experiences was over and now it was time to move on. I was somewhat uncomfortable with the unknown and was afraid of being duped by an occasional fraudulent medium, psychic or teacher with their hand out with an offer (for a price) to help me share the divine aspects of my journey. Anyway, during our last session, Leianne put me into a trance and directed that I call for my spirit guide to visit. By this point, I was a little skeptical and did not believe myself to be in an altered state at all. Despite my skepticism, a man appeared in my mind's eye.

I was surprised, to say the least. I did not recognize this man. I marveled at this image and the fact that I didn't know him. His face was long, and he had dark hair and a stern expression. He was there looking at me as I looked at him. As mentioned previously, I always knew somebody was watching over me; here he was, but I still had absolutely no clue who he was. That would come a few months later, also unexpectedly.

While I am sure Leianne directed me to ask questions and have a dialogue with him, I don't remember it. But I do remember the image of his face. It was my guardian angel who has protected me my entire life; protected me from being psychologically damaged by witnessing my father's abuse of my mother, living in fear and being put down and criticized for simply being who I was. Later in life, when I went through a period when I was tempted to make very bad decisions, he was there ensuring I didn't. And he is still with me, although I would like to think he doesn't have to work so hard now!

Chapter Seven

A VISIT WITH REBECCA ROSEN
MARCH 16, 2011

Quinton's Lesson: Expect the unexpected.

Kristine and I belong to a fraternity of parents whose children have transitioned to the other side. One member of this group of friends is Cathee Lecount, who lost her 16-year-old daughter (Mara Parslow) to a car accident on January 6, 2010, at Shaffer's Crossing on Highway 285 between Conifer and Pine Junction. Because this is a small community in the foothills of Colorado (just west of Denver), we ended up meeting Cathee during the spring of 2010. Our journey had already begun; we had already seen and heard Quinton through visions, which sent us down a new path of understanding and learning.

Part of our path included visiting with a psychic who told us amazing things from Quinton and predictions of the future that have since come to pass. As we got to know Cathee, we shared books we each had read on life after death and metaphysics. One day, she shared the difference between a psychic and a medium; she shared that a psychic typically gets a sense of our transitioned loved one, while a medium actually makes direct contact with our loved one. She told us about a local medium named Rebecca Rosen who had written a book titled *Spirited*, and said she did group readings. This sounded exciting. But at that moment, it wasn't high on our list of priorities.

We continued to receive visits and signs from Quinton, and late in 2010, I Googled Rebecca Rosen, (www.rebeccarosen.com) and signed up to be on her mailing list to receive notices of upcoming sessions. Almost immediately afterward, Carol Rowe, a co-worker at Prime West, gave me her copy of *Spirited*. Talk about synchronicity! Both Kristine and I read the book as we waited for the dates of two sessions we planned to attend. The first one occurred on February 24, 2011. It was standing room only.

I was amazed by Rebecca as she stood on the stage alone in front of 330 people determining who in the crowd belonged to the voices in her head. This was a tough venue, but she plugged away for more than two hours, and those who heard from transitioned loved ones were visibly moved.

Quinton didn't come through on this visit; we tried not to be disappointed as we bought our own copy of *Spirited* and then had dinner in the restaurant above the venue. As we finished our meal, Kristine noticed that Rebecca was still there, so we hopped in line and had our book signed. She said she noticed us meditating in the crowd, and we smiled and chatted with her as we appreciated her energy. We didn't mention Quinton, knowing we would see her again on March 16 for a small group reading consisting of only 12 people.

March 16 came quickly. After picking Kristine up at a bus stop not far from our home in Conifer, we made our way to Cherry Creek where the reading would take place in Rebecca's office. We grabbed a quick dinner at a Chinese restaurant just around the corner from our final destination. While at dinner, Kristine asked me to tighten a screw on her sunglasses; I tried but only was able to get the screw in partially. As we walked to Rebecca's office, we mentally catalogued our transitioned family members; naturally, our focus was on Quinton, but we had read enough James Van Praagh and Silvia Browne books to know that anyone might stop in for a visit. Still, we were completely unprepared for what was to come.

Quinton's Legacy

We arrived and were ushered into a room in the office on the third floor. A professional production team was present to videotape the entire session and, as always, Rebecca was digitally recording the entire session for everyone who attended. After a quick meditation, the session began. We sat there, trying to be relaxed and attentive. The room was warm and time seemed to pass slowly, but in retrospect the two-hour session went quickly.

At the beginning of the session, Rebecca said there were three children under the age of 30 who had passed who were there, and she asked who had children who had passed. Neither Kristine nor I said anything, as we wanted something more concrete. In the past, we told psychics about Quinton, but we wanted Rebecca to discover Quinton on her own, so we were not giving hints. We might have missed an opportunity here as Rebecca continued to share spirit messages and worked around the room. Thirty-five minutes passed and nothing from Quinton. We were starting to wonder if we would hear from our son, and we were trying to be okay with it. We told ourselves, if nothing else, we were taking part in an amazing experience as we witnessed so many incredible connections others were having.

The first time George was mentioned, we were 35 minutes into the reading; nobody knew a George that had passed. Thirty-eight minutes into the reading George was back and still no takers, and then Kristine remembered that she had an Uncle George who passed away. "Uncle George also went by the name of Uncle Weno."

"The next the image I'm getting is a bottle of Jack Daniels." Rebecca didn't seem to think the connection was for us. She went around the room again.

She asked the gentleman who told the group he was a recovering alcoholic, "Did you and your father drink Jack Daniels?

He responded, "We drank everything together," but it was clear that the Jack Daniels reference wasn't a connection for him.

At that point Kristine spoke up again, "Uncle George used to own a bar." Rebecca was now sure that this spirit was for Kristine. "During his life he also owned a security company."

"For this reading he is the gatekeeper, responsible for opening the door for all of the family members and friends to follow." I was awestruck hearing this information.

The first to come through after Uncle George was Betty Boop. It took Kristine a second or two, then she remembered, "Yes, this must be a friend of the family who took care of me when I was little." Kristine, little as she was, used to pin Betty's hair up in such a way that it reminded her of Betty Boop, so when the reference came up it made perfect sense.

"I see an image of her kissing you, Kristine. Right on your forehead, which means you were always very special to her." She paused as if listening to something we could not hear, "Someone else is here who is a diabetic."

"It's my father Ed Cano." Ed transitioned on June 8, 2003 from a massive heart attack.

"He's happy and says he's eating every piece of candy he can get his hands on." After a moment, she smiled, "Ed is amazed that this is finally happening. He's delighted to be part of the reading and is sharing a feeling of gratitude with me; he's been waiting to make contact with you."

As if she was changing the subject, she asked, "Does the number 11 have any significance, either November or the 11th?" It didn't. "I hear the name Chuck."

Kristine remembered, "This is my Uncle Charlie who transitioned last week. He's my dad's brother." It warmed her heart to know that Ed and his brother Charlie were together.

"Ed is showing me socks or shoes." We didn't understand. "Ed says he is 'free' and as light as a feather." This made sense because we knew all too well of his health issues. "He's sending me an image of a Tootsie Roll, and he wants you to know that if you see one, it's a sign from him. He also says to send love to mom." We knew that he was talking about his wife Nellie.

To our amazement, the line of family members continued. "I'm getting the impression of a teacher or educator with an RO in his name."

"This must be Uncle Ronnie, another of Ed's brothers." We were amazed that all three of them were together in spirit for this reading. But the then Ed spoke up with a puzzling joke about his mouth.

"It's his dentures," Kristine finally remembered.

"His teeth are no longer a problem." Continuing, Rebecca turned to me so that Ed could speak to me directly, "Thank you, Ernie, for everything you are doing for my daughter Kristine. You are more than a husband. You're also a caregiver and father figure. He says he is sending you gratitude as his son; he thinks of you as a son."

This was all so amazing, I mean totally over the top; we were filled with a sense of awe! While we thought Ed might come through, we had absolutely no idea how much of our family he would bring with him. From 38 minutes into the recording to minute 50, it was about our loved ones. It came so quick and truly was mind blowing. We were even more amazed when we listened to the recording the following day. As the reading continued, my grandfather came through. Rebecca said, "I'm getting the sense that either you have never met this man, or you only knew him when you were a small child." I assumed that it was my paternal grandfather, but in hindsight, it may have been my maternal grandfather.

"He is saluting you, and he says he is your guardian angel. He's telling me you have a mouth of gold and can talk yourself into and out of anything. He stays with you to keep you out of trouble. He also says your integrity is strong – you have a good soul and serve others." Rebecca continued, "He feels you are on point, doing what you are supposed to be doing. You're on the right track. He hopes that you walk away from this reading feeling good about who you are and that you are of service to others."

I felt humbled, but still didn't know which grandfather he was. And more spirits came.

Rebecca continued, "A man named Jack is coming through. Who knows a Jack?"

Kristine whispered in my ear, "That's Jack Childs." This was even more unexpected. Jack died of a heart attack while at the airport in September of 2001, before the terrorist attacks on the World Trade Center.

Rebecca asked who Jack Childs was and I said, "Jack was a very close family friend."

"Jack says he is honored to pop in here to say hello. He's been a little frustrated with the lack of closure to his life but now is at peace knowing that he is where he's supposed to be." And just that quick, he was gone from the reading.

"Ed is back and wants to talk about his body. Was Ed having physical issues when he passed?"

"Yes," Kristine said, "Ed lost two toes to diabetes before he was called home." This must be related to the socks and shoes comment, as Ed rarely wore socks when he was around the house.

"He is in awe of the fact that he still exists. He says he has been reviewing his book of life. He needed to struggle to grow in this lifetime but he assures you that he visits all three of his children equally (Kristine, Julie and Ed Jr.). Then Rebecca looked at me, "Do you have a fun car?

"Yes, but I drove it into the ground and sold it."

"Ed says you'll get a fun car." Then she explained, "Our loved ones are not interested in material things, but Ed wants you to play, to have fun, to bring out your inner child."

Then she looked at both of us, "Have you been to Hawaii?"

"We haven't, but Kristine and I have been talking about it."

"Ed says you should go. He says that the trip may be gifted to us in some way, maybe through a tax refund. Uncle Ronnie is now saying hello to you."

"There's a lot of spirit activity in your home trying to get your attention." She paused again as if she was looking at something new. "They're showing me something about hanging up pictures."

Neither Kristine nor I knew what to make of that comment until I remembered, "Yes, we made a calendar with many images of Quinton and ordered three copies. When the package arrived in the mail, I opened it, saw what it was and left it on the counter for Kristine. But when she woke up, one of the three calendars was hanging up. Realizing neither of us hung it up, we wondered who hung it."

"It was the spirits," Rebecca told us. Later we discovered that Cheyanne hung the calendar, but since she would never do this on her own, we knew she'd been inspired. This explains her unusual behavior.

Rebecca continued, "Ed is back once again. He's saying the nickname Kiki or Ceci."

"He's referring to our nephew, his grandson, TK."

"Ed watches over TK, and he's mentioning his broken phone."

Kristine confirmed Ed's statement, "TK lost the back of his cell phone a few days ago."

"Ed wants you to know that TK senses energy, and if he mentions feeling grandpa, validate him."

This is what I mean about a direct connection to spirit. The skeptic in all of us wonders what is real. In working with mediums, we look for the validating comment; information that comes through that could not possibly be known. For example, there is no way Rebecca could know about TK, no way at all.

Rebecca still had more for us. "Are you adding on to your home?" Neither Kristine nor I knew what she was referring to. We had remodeled in 2007 to make room for TK. While we didn't have any intentions of adding any interior living space, I had been toying with possible re-siding or extending the deck farther to wrap around the front of the house and add a porch, which probably qualifies as adding on.

"Ed is saying not to add on. Don't spend the money. He's telling me that it would be better off relocating at some point in the future. He's sending an image of Miami. Have you been in Florida?"

Kristine responded, "We were in Orlando recently."

"Were you thinking of Ed?"

"Yes!"

"Ed said that he was there with you." This was yet another validating comment. I could tell Rebecca wanted to move on to the others as she was spending so much more time with us, but she closed by saying, "Ed loves you both unconditionally and eternally. He is sending you an image of roses." Then she directed her comments to me, "Your take-away from this session is that you now know that your grandfather helps you and is working with you."

And we were through, or so we thought.

For the next hour or so Rebecca went around the room sharing messages for others, while Kristine and I sat there wondering when and if Quinton would be coming. Near the end of the session, Rebecca asked "Is there anyone who hasn't heard from a loved one they wanted to hear from?"

I raised my hand. "No, I have not heard from who I wanted to hear from," which must have seemed odd given how many of our loved ones came through for us. One other person said the same thing, so Rebecca concentrated to see who might still be out there trying to contact us.

She turned to me, "Your father is here." I really didn't expect him. My father played a large role in my life by, shall we say, showing me how I *didn't* want to live my life. I did what I could (during his later life) to show him a different path, but it was apparently too late for him to change. My path was not his, and his was not for me; we agreed to disagree and went our separate ways. He died on September 25, 2003.

Rebecca asked, "Did you have a brother or a father who died young?

"My father died in his 60s, not long after he turned 67.

"I'm getting a choking sensation – not being able to breath."

"We were told he died of a heart attack."

"I'm seeing the letter J."

"His last name was Jackson and middle name James, but as a youth, his nickname was Junior."

Rebecca was now certain that this was my father. "Your dad feels you need to know about his death. He said that he couldn't breathe; that he panicked – it felt like someone was sitting on his chest. After he left his body, it took him a week to cross over."

"That makes sense because it took five days for his body to be discovered."

Next Rebecca asked, "Did he have a nickname?"

"His given name was Ernest, but he went by Ernie."

We said "Ernie" at almost the same time. "I got the image of the Sesame Street characters, Bert and Ernie, and that's your name, too."

"This isn't the first time I had heard that one."

"Your dad is very proud of you, and he wants you to know that he is relaxing. I see an image of him having a drink."

In that moment, I missed the point entirely. The mention of him having a drink dredged up old memories of his addictive personality, but Rebecca seemed to understand my thoughts and stayed the course, "The image of the drink simply means he's relaxing."

"He said that he was not the kind of father who guided you or helped you through life; he served a different role in your life. He wants you to know that he's very proud of you for doing better than him.

Now I'm seeing an image of a pair of glasses."

We couldn't figure it out until Kristine remembered, "Ernie had been trying to fix my glasses at the restaurant before we came to the reading."

"That's it. He wants to let you know that he was there watching you at the restaurant."

"Now he's sending an image of a baseball card. Do you know what that is about?

"I'm not sure, but we used to play catch."

"Did he ever say he was good at playing baseball?"

"Yes," I confirmed that he had and knew this was one more validation that he was there.

"He's showing me an image of you being together in the mountains."

"We live in the mountains," I offered. But later, after listening to the recording for a third time, I understood the significance of that image. Often, we would go fishing at Jefferson Lake or Echo Lake, both in the mountains of Colorado; we both enjoyed these times together.

Rebecca continued, "Sometimes your father sends a sign through a whiff of smoke."

He used to enjoy smoking cigarettes and pipes during his lifetime, but this sign is actually quite hilarious since I can't stand the smell of smoke. I guess I will have to accept that this is how my father lets me know he is near.

"Does anyone have metal in their body, like pins in their knees?"

"I have titanium in my shoulder," I remembered.

I've got the image of setting off the metal detectors in airports."

I laughed and said, "I do."

"Your father is teasing you about that. Again, he is telling me that he is proud of you, and added that he is trying to evolve, but he could not be your guide." Rebecca added, "Your grandfather is your guide."

"But I didn't know my grandfather."

"You don't have to. In fact, not knowing him allows him to guide you. Since he couldn't be your guide in life, he is your guide now."

The session ended, but Quinton still hadn't come through.

We all stood up and started milling around looking at the books and audiotapes that Rebecca was selling. Kristine decided to purchase another copy of *Spirited* while I headed out of the now very warm room. While on my way out, one of the recording crew asked me if we could stay so they could speak to Kristine and me about our experience during the reading.

Afterward, I looked at Rebecca's personal library and noted the books we have both read while Kristine stood in line to get her book autographed. Rebecca noticed Kristine's necklace, a charm that contained a picture of both of our children. In response to Rebecca's attention to the pendant, Kristine said, "Tell our son, hello and that we miss him if you happen to hear from him." Rebecca had been introduced to many of our relatives on the other side, but now understood that we had lost our son.

After Rebecca signed the book, Kristine met me in the outer room where we sat together and, not long after that, Rebecca came out and sat with us. I commented on her library and Kristine added that I was looking for a new book to read. After recommending *Journey of Souls* by Michael Newton, she changed topics.

"You lost your son?" she asked.

"Yes."

As she sat there across from us she asked, "Do you remember that when the reading started that there were three children trying to come through?"

"Yes."

"The third child was your son. He was very light, and it was hard to get to his essence, as he is an old soul. Did you almost lose him between the ages of six and eight?"

Kristine and I looked at each other. I almost forgot, yet nobody knew this; yet another validating comment. "Quinton caught a cold when he was seven years old and couldn't breathe. Kristine took him to the doctor, and when they checked his blood oxygen, they immediately called an ambulance."

"He was supposed to die then, and the time you had with him afterward was bonus time. Do you still have his remains?"

"We do."

Quinton is telling me that he wants you to spread his remains sometime between the third and fourth anniversary of his transition, and that you already know this place."

I was thinking he meant the Four Corners area where we lost him, but then Rebecca was given the image of a dolphin."

"It's clear he means Rocky Point."

"He wants you to tell Neiko hello and to let him know that he enjoyed playing with him."

Kristine and I looked at each other. I didn't have a clue what he was referring to, but Kristine knew. When Cheyanne was in junior high school, her boyfriend's name was Nick. Quinton and Nick got along very well, and Quinton's nickname for Nick was Neiko. Talk about validation! Quinton was indeed there with us and came through to Rebecca. This was incredible!

Validation, or a validating comment, is an important part of working with a medium, because for so many of us, our hearts are skeptical. In the world today, how could you not be? Spirit knows this all too well, and will say or show something through the medium so that we know they are really connecting with those on the other side. The medium becomes the conduit between sides. In Rebecca Rosen's book *Spirited*, she wrote,

One afternoon with Dad and Seth that summer, I was playing around with automatic writing when a spirit named 'Larry' came through. I couldn't think of anyone that my dad or I knew by that name, so I asked Seth, 'Do you know anyone named Larry?' He was dumbfounded. 'That's my father,' he said. 'He's been dead a long time.' 'Well,' I said, 'he's telling me that he's very sorry about his sudden death and how it tore the family apart. He also wants me to mention the briefcase.' Seth stared at me with tears in his eyes. He then confided in me that his father had died when Seth was just a teenager. The only thing that he still had of his father's was his briefcase (Rosen, Rebecca, *Spirited*, page 22, 2010, Harper Collins Publishers, 10 East 53rd Street, New York, NY).

This is a wonderful example of a validating comment. Our reading was riddled with validation, especially our private session with Rebecca when Quinton came through. The comment about Neiko embodies what a validating comment was supposed to do; nobody knew this about Nick and Neiko, certainly not Rebecca – this was not public information.

After the reading with Rebecca, I was stuck trying to figure out which grandfather was my guardian angel. While I thought it could be my paternal grandfather because at least I had met him, my intuition told me otherwise. After a short time I asked my mom for a picture of her father. She didn't have any pictures and since she hadn't lived with him, it would be a challenge to get one. Mom and I discussed it a couple of times, but then I let it go, putting it into the hands of the universe to connect the dots if they were meant to be connected.

It took a while because my mom had to work through a friend of the family, but she finally got her hands on some pictures and sent me one. I was totally blown away when the picture arrived. My maternal grandfather's name was Jack, and it was his face that came to my mind during my last session with my life-coach Leianne Wilson. It is mind boggling to finally put the pieces together. A lifetime is a wondrous journey, and it never ceases to amaze me what I learn along the way.

It took so many years for the identity of my guardian angel to be revealed. Along that journey I had hints, like breadcrumbs for me to follow, once my consciousness had been pierced. Looking back, I have always been guided; from my early years where I knew that I was being protected by something non-physical–something external to me–to the realizations and epiphanies that came to me in later years. Looking back, many examples come to mind: when I heard a voice telling me at 27 that I would be a good father; or the realization that it was time to sell the family janitorial business because I needed to have more challenging experiences in my life; or wondering why I was sheltered from death for so long after so many instances of reckless driving.

Finally, I envisioned (during light hypnosis) the face of a man in my mind's eye when asked to see my guardian angel. Here was a man I have never met before, and now know it is he who has been protecting me in my life. What amazing knowledge to have! I know I have more to learn and more to do to further evolve my spirit. What a journey!

See picture of my grandpa, Jack Cleaton (second from the upper right).

Note to the reader: During Quinton's visit with us via the medium Rebecca Rosen, he sent an image of a dolphin in reference to where he wanted his ashes spread. Up to this point, I don't recall ever having seen a dolphin while on our annual vacation to Rocky Point. But two-and-a-half months later, while on the beach in Rocky Point, I saw dolphins – several times – frolicking in the water not far from the shore. And in my excitement, I jumped up and down pointing and shouting, "Dolphins, dolphins!" Thanks Q – got it, on so many levels!

Section Two

Recognizing Signs

Chapter Eight

SIGNS AND VISITATIONS

Quinton's Lesson: Pay Attention!

Death sucks! I don't have to tell you this! Losing a loved one to death is what all of us must and will face, but that doesn't make it any easier. It doesn't matter if it is a parent, sibling or child; it sucks all the same. It's devastating for us because we are left here with holes in our hearts that can't ever be filled. While this is our predicament, we must never lose sight that our loved ones are in heaven and continue to exist on the other side without pain, fear or doubt. Our loved ones continue to exist within a field of unconditional love! And here is the kicker; we'll do the same when we transition! This applies to everyone.

You may or may not believe this, but one thing is certain, we continue to live after we leave these temporary shells. How can I be so certain, you may ask? I am certain because our loved ones make contact with us, or at least attempt to do so after they cross the threshold to the other side. These signs and visits come in many forms, so don't get hung up on the details; there are no rules! Anything that makes you take pause and say things like, "that was odd," "that was unusual," "that was weird," or even "that was so strange, it just never happened before," could very well be your deceased loved one attempting to let his/her presence be known *from the other side.* These visits are often dismissed as coincidence or imagination; we may be too busy to notice. Sometimes the signs are so subtle we miss them. It often takes a quiet mind, but not always – even this is not an absolute truth. Just pay attention with an open heart. Suspend your disbelief and your judgment. On the other hand, sometimes our loved ones come through so forcefully, even the most skeptical person knows exactly what is going on.

Quinton came through to me in several different ways; none that I expected. I wasn't looking for signs because I had no clue, in that moment, that visitations even were possible. I certainly did not expect this. I was too numb, struggling to process the fact that my son was dead, to even be in the mindset to look for him. So when the first sign came a mere 30 hours *after* Quinton "died," I didn't realize it was him.

As I lay in bed, trying to sleep for the first time since the accident, I felt my left hand being held. Of that I had no doubt – I knew my hand was being held; it was real and beyond question! I actually remember thinking to myself, "This must be the manifestation of all the prayers coming our way," as I tried to understand who was holding my hand. My prayers continued and amplified over the coming days, but I never felt that sensation again. As I observed from a higher perspective over the following weeks, I realized it must have been Quinton holding my hand! I shared a bit of this in *Quinton's Messages,* and a friend called me on it. She asked, "Well, how do you know it was Quinton?" Aside from the simple answer "I just know," I replied, "Quinton had the softest hands, and we all loved holding his hands. He knew that he could get through to me this way!"

Sometimes our loved ones make contact via another person, and we get the information second hand. This is quite common. As I wrote in *Quinton's Messages,* five days after Quinton crossed over, messages came via a medicine man. When Chris Voldrich shared her encounter with the medicine man, my consciousness was pierced. My son lives! What a glorious moment for me, after Quinton's death, when he revealed that he is still alive. Talk about a silver lining!

We have a couple of dear friends who lost a son in the Columbine tragedy in 1999 (mere months before Quinton was born). They shared with us that not only did their son visit, but the majority of the parents who lost children in that awful tragedy also had visits from their children. Can you imagine the group of them getting together to grieve and cry, then one person shares a visit, then another and before too long all of them are exchanging details of the visits from their deceased children! I fully expect this scene has been carried out time and time again after various tragedies.

When Quinton passed, I knew I would wear one of his earrings. I lost the one he was wearing during his transition; I guess he wanted it for himself! One day, while cleaning my pierced ear in the mirror after a shower, I saw Quinton in his room while I looked in the mirror. He seemed taller and was walking from west to east in his room. I turned around and went into his room to see who was there, but the room was empty. I stood in his doorway with my mouth open.

There are no rules. I am not the least bit surprised that he was somewhat taller. I still knew it was Quinton. To this day, while Kristine puts on her make-up in her mirror, she sees him in the background of her peripheral vision. If she looks toward him, he is gone, but he is there in her peripheral vision. While attending a meeting at the Parents United in Loss (Helping Parents Heal) support group (www. helpingparentsheal.info), co-founded by Elizabeth Boisson and author Mark Ireland, in Scottsdale Arizona on March 17, 2013, we learned that what we both experienced, and in Kristine's case still experiences, is called mirror gazing. This phenomenon was first shared by Plato over 2,300 years ago. Dr. Raymond Moody also discusses it in his book *Reunions: Visionary Encounters with Departed Loved Ones.* Our loved ones still exist, still live, just on the other side!

Later that summer of 2009, I heard Quinton call my name one morning as I walked down the hall while everyone else in the house slept. As I passed Quinton's room, I heard, "Dad!" I didn't expect this one either, and it only happened once. I was caught so off guard that I didn't know what to do. I smiled to myself in acknowledgement of what had just occurred, but could not think fast enough to shout, "Quinton, what's up son? Tell me how you have been and what you have been doing." Our loved ones still exist!

In October, a full four months after Quinton crossed the threshold, he came to me in a vision. I struggle to remember my dreams; they are fuzzy and quickly forgotten when I arise and usually come during the night. My visions, or more mystical experiences or visitations, are different. They are crystal clear and unforgettable. They seem real and come to me at odd times, like between 5:00 a.m. and 7:00 a.m. Friends, there are no rules! While this is how it works for me, as far as the times are concerned, it doesn't mean it is the only way. Visions and visitations may come at any time; even an unexplained crystal clear image of your deceased loved one popping in your mind's eye, or remembering something that reminds you of them, is also a sign. There are no rules!

The visitation from Quinton, which I started to share, was crystal clear. In my vision, I saw Quinton's shadow at my feet. He was above me on the deck of our second story home in Conifer. I knew it was Quinton. As I turned, still within the grasp of his visit, I expected him to dissolve before I laid my eyes on him, but this time he didn't! I saw his face for the first time since he had left us in the physical realm four months prior. I could see what he was wearing, the length of his hair and even the expressions on his face. I called out his name repeatedly in joy! And so began my rapid journey back to consciousness. Before I awoke, he jumped off the deck above me. And as I opened my eyes, I felt myself catch him – he merged with me. I was filled with the most amazing sense of calm and peace, a feeling that I have never felt before. Now I associate that deep sense of calm with Quinton. When it overtakes me, I get goose bumps because I know it's him.

In 2014, I found myself part of the Arizona Holistic Chamber of Commerce's committee to plan and coordinate its Second Death and Dying Conference, which took place in Scottsdale, Arizona. I was honored to share my perspective with six others on the committee while looking for the right people to present at the conference. To my surprise, there were many speakers to choose from, as this information is everywhere. Don't believe me? Just Google "signs from our deceased loved ones" and begin your own search. Enjoy your journey.

Suddenly, for me, the word *lifetime* took on an entirely different meaning!

Quinton made his presence known to us in waking hours and in sleeping visions. As I shared in *Quinton's Messages*, within three days after the accident, my friend and brother, John McDonough was inspired to write this poem:

> In an instant,
> in the beat of a hummingbird's wing,
> faster than the blink of an eye . . .
> nothing will ever be the same.
> There is only before and after
> that moment in time.
> Before is a gift that no one can steal;
> After is a choice, a story yet to be written.
> To not create a beautiful tomorrow
> would be like throwing away
> all of the yesterdays.
> Today, I cannot see that future;
> the dark clouds that surround
> yet comfort me
> block out that sky,
> that rainbow after the storm,
> beaconing me toward tomorrow.

On Sunday, June 21, 2009, 30 friends gathered in our yard to perform a planting ceremony to dedicate a nine-foot spruce tree they had purchased to celebrate Quinton's nine years of life. During that ceremony, a solitary hummingbird hovered motionless directly over the tree. Almost everyone saw it. And since John's poem was on the prayer cards handed out at the service, everyone immediately recognized the significance of the hummingbird. We knew Quinton was there! A skeptic might think this was merely a coincidence, or the result of an overactive imagination, but everyone who saw the hummingbird that day knew exactly what was happening.

As the summer days of 2009 passed, the hummingbirds continued to get our attention. Kristine noted that one day, as she stood on the landing outside our front door, a hummingbird came up to her face and hovered 12 inches directly in front of her at eye level, just looking at her. On another occasion, a hummingbird knocked itself out trying to fly into the house through a closed window. I sat outside with the unconscious hummingbird in my hand, gently caressing it with my index finger until it suddenly woke up and flew way. It perched in a tree nearby, where there it sat looking back at us.

We are not the only ones who've had unusual hummingbird experiences. While attending the St. Baldrick's fundraising event, a Denver group that raises funds to eradicate childhood cancer, we spoke to a man who lost his son to cancer. He wore a shirt honoring his transitioned son and on the shirt was an image of a hummingbird. I asked the significance and he indicated they acted "odd" after his son died, so now hummingbirds remind them of his son.

I've heard so many hummingbird stories from those who have had loved ones transition; I am unable to remember them all. But here's one of my favorites. After sharing our journey at the Boulder Bookstore on April 22, 2013, a tall, middle-aged man approached me. He told me that his father passed, he was sitting outdoors and felt something touch his left ear. Three times he brushed it away, but after the third time he turned and saw a hummingbird quietly hovering inches from him. Then the hummingbird moved to a point directly in front of him – at eye level – hovered for 15 or 20 seconds before making the sign of the cross while in flight and then flew away. He said he doesn't usually share that story, but felt moved to tell me about it. What is even more "interesting" was that during my 25-minute presentation, not once did I mention our experiences with hummingbirds!

Remember what I said previously; don't get hung up on expectations or other people's experiences. In other words, **there are no rules!** For you, odd behavior might be exhibited by a butterfly landing on your shoulder, then landing on your big toe, all the while looking at you. Anything that seems odd, unusual, weird, interesting, or something that you have never witnessed before could very well be a sign. Is it a stretch to think like this? Well, maybe other people in your life who aren't as receptive may think so, but the experience is for you, not them! Your transitioned loved one is be trying to comfort you by making contact to let **YOU** know that they *live* and that they are doing all right.

Another potential sign of a loved one's presence is when a light turns off or on with no explanation. Much has been written about how many of our deceased loved ones attempt to contact us by manipulating electricity. Kristine and I continue to have electrical signs. When we walk our dogs or even take a drive in the evening, often while near a streetlamp, it will suddenly turn off. This happens all the time. All the time! Normally, this is easy to chalk up to coincidence, but the fact that it happens so often has taken the "coincidence" totally out of our minds. One week late in April 2013, while I walked the dogs alone, a streetlight suddenly went black on the way home. I stopped in gratitude, saying Hi to Quinton. As I continued home, a neighbor cat began to follow us, so we stopped. This cat I never "knew" came right up to us and let me pet it. Coincidence? You can think so, but I *know* otherwise.

A few nights later, another streetlight went off, this time behind me. As I turned to the blackened streetlight to acknowledge the sign, I noticed a cloud in the western sky in the shape of a dolphin with a perfect dorsal fin and snout. While this dolphin reference probably means nothing to anyone else, it is a direct reference to a message that

Quinton sent to us via a well-known medium, Rebecca Rosen, in April of 2011. The sign was personal and amazing.

My point is that anything can be a sign. There are no rules, and the experiences of others may not be relevant to you. A sign or a visit is designed to be very personal; only you get it. Interestingly, because the signs are so personal, many of us don't share our experience with others.

Chapter Nine

ANOTHER LEAP OF FAITH AND AN AMAZING SIGN

Quinton's Lesson: Spirit can help us!

I came home late in September 2012 with purpose. I had been working at Prime West since October 2010 – a dream job for me. My amazing boss, Karen Cerny, allowed me to do my job without restrictions, and the owner, Franklin Street Properties, loved the results. My asset manager, Will Friend, is one of the best people I've ever worked for. It was a wonderful job, but the signs pointed me in a different direction.

Kristine's tolerance of the cold was continuing to diminish, due to the injuries sustained in the accident that took our dear son, Quinton. She endured three winters in Conifer since the accident; each was progressively worse in terms of the numbing pain caused by the cold. She rarely complained, standing by my side, even though doing so caused her so much discomfort. Often at night, in an effort to stop the tingly nerve and arthritic pain, she took a hot shower, sat by our wood stove at 800 degrees (as hot as we dare run it), before climbing into our bed piled with blankets.

Another winter was looming and now I was having pain, too. For six months, my lower back hurt so bad that, at times, it was difficult to walk. I drove an hour to work. When I arrived, I would carefully get out of our Hyundai Sonata and then stand on one foot while trying to get the feeling back into my right leg, then limp into the office. I started physical therapy, and my wonderful team at Prime West converted my desk into a stand-up workstation; both helped with the pain situation, but then I noticed something else that nobody who knows me would understand.

While the physical pain was decreasing, I slowly became aware that during my drives home I was angry. Well, to be completely honest, I was in a rage. Oddly enough, there was nothing for me to be upset about; everything was great at work, home and with the family. And there wasn't anything in particular happening during any given day to annoy me. My rage was baseless, but it was there just the same.

True to my normal patterns, this rage traveled with me for a couple of weeks before I even recognized it was a problem. But when I did, I was alarmed. Once I acknowledged it, I had the presence of mind to stop it in mid-imaginary rant long enough to understand its basis. Then one day at its onset, I began to imagine a different life; a scenario where I wasn't driving an hour twice a day, going back and forth from work. The rage vanished, immediately!

I felt like an Indian tracker looking for signs, looking for a path that I was supposed to be taking. With me, I am ashamed to say, usually pain and anger are signs that something is amiss. They are the fuel to propel me down a different path. The one time this wasn't the case was when Quinton passed. That's when awe and wonder propelled me to take a leap of faith that lead to me resigning from Schnitzer West and to write *Quinton's Messages*.

My rage abated immediately after realizing it was time for a change. Shortly thereafter, I told Kristine I was going to resign from Prime West so I could spend more time working on this book, the sequel to *Quinton's Messages*, and develop a speaking career. I wanted to share the lessons we've learned from Quinton's departure from the physical realm. She humored me as we discussed telling our daughter, Cheyanne and T.K., our nephew who lived with us. Kristine thought I was pulling her leg. For 14 years, she heard me say how much I loved Conifer, how much I loved being in the Front Range foothills of Colorado. So she didn't believe me until I told her I had an appointment with my boss Karen to discuss our plans and provide her with a 90-day notice. That's when she knew I was serious and asked, "Don't you think that is a little soon?" But part of me knew how difficult leaving would be, so I wanted to initiate the change before I changed my mind!

We discussed finding renters for our Conifer home and began doing the legwork to find the best company to assist us in our efforts. Kristine worked on the house arrangements while I met with Karen the following week. Shortly thereafter, as I was telling the management team at Prime West how honored I was to be associated with them and of our plans to move to Arizona, the thought suddenly came to me that we should put the house on the market. What did we have to lose in doing so? And it would provide us with another option besides renting the home.

I have a tendency to be spontaneous, so I texted Cathie Nicholson (our realtor friend) on the spot, telling her my thoughts. I told Kristine later that afternoon when I spoke with her; I figured she wouldn't object since I knew she was excited to be moving back to the warmth of Arizona. I was right. Yes, maybe I should have discussed it with her first, but the spirit whispered in my ear and I felt moved to act and act quickly. Thirty days after the house went on the market, it sold!

This turn of events was exciting and scary at the same time. While understanding this was the correct course of action, the prospect of leaving the mountain community I had loved for so many years loomed in the back of my mind. At this point though, the pace of change had gone beyond a simple sprint; we were running as fast as we could to dispose of our possessions and meet with as many friends as possible before leaving.

For my part, I just took my books, my roll-top desk, some movies, music and clothes. Still, we had our bed, my extra set of tires for Q's truck and knick-knacks. As the December 10, 2012 closing date fast approached, we began to realize we had run out of time. We went to U-Haul to rent a five-by-eight-foot trailer, only to get there and realize it was too small. So we picked up a dual axel, six-by-twelve-foot trailer. Upon arriving home, we started packing it. As we loaded, we asked our friends to come by and take whatever they wanted from a substantial list of things we weren't taking. Our Phoenix house was fully furnished, so there was little that we needed to take with us, and we were happy to share with friends.

We closed on the tenth, stuffing the remaining odds and ends into the trailer until well after sunset. Troy and Cathie Nicholson saved the day yet again by taking load after load of stuff we didn't need. And then it was time to go. Driving up the driveway for the last time was bittersweet – of that there is no doubt.

This was Quinton's home we were pulling away from, the only earthly home he ever knew; even through three-and-a-half years passed since his transition, this wasn't easy; so many memories and so much love. And yet, we knew Quinton was watching and keeping tabs on us. He would demonstrate that in a spectacular fashion by weeks' end. Our friends Lynn and Shelly Koglin graciously agreed to let us stay in their home in Louisville, not far from where I worked in Broomfield. We pulled up the driveway and turned left into the cul-de-sac. Then we backed the packed trailer into the driveway of our neighbors Rob and Mindy Johns, unhitched and then drove to Louisville.

The week was filled with excitement and passed in a blur. The house sold on the tenth, but I agreed to work until the fourteenth. As my last day of employment with Prime West approached, and we prepared to leave, we kept an eye on the weather. A storm was brewing southwest of us in the Four Corners region, and I was trying to decide the best course of action; staying in Denver beyond December 14 was not one of the options in my mind. I was trying to decide whether or not to go south on I-25 or risk taking Highway 285 over Wolf Creek pass with the thought that we would be spending Quinton's birthday in Phoenix.

December 14 dawned, and I headed to the office for one last time as an employee of Prime West. As a part of my going away party, the team got to taste my fried chicken – a dish I had been bragging about for the whole 26 months I'd worked there. At last I was making it for them. I brought in a deep fryer and cooked it right there at the office. Kristine and Cheyanne arrived during the lunch hour along with Karen, our realtor. The term bittersweet fits this dichotomy of emotions to a T; they were going to miss me, and I was going to miss them. There was laughter, tears and lots of storytelling; then it was time to go.

Cheyanne headed home to her apartment, and we drove to the Koglin's to load up our truck and drive west to pick up the trailer tucked away in the cul-de-sac at the end of Griffin Drive in Conifer. We reached the trailer just after 4:00 p.m.; the sun was still up and the sky was mostly blue. At this point, I decided we would take Highway 285 toward Wolf Creek pass. I asked Kristine to call for lodging in South Fork as I proceeded to get the truck lined up with the trailer. Then a funny thing happened. The transmission went out on our 2009, 2500 mega-cab Dodge pickup with a Cummins diesel engine that we had been driving with no problems since we purchased it. I put the transmission into reverse and backed up toward the trailer, but it wasn't lined up straight. After stopping and shifting into drive, I noticed the transmission was stuck in what seemed to be a super low gear. I went back and forth a few times hoping that something would change, but it didn't. We weren't going anywhere.

We called AAA and then decided the best course of action. The tow truck wouldn't be there for a while, so we called Cheyanne and asked her to pick us up. Meanwhile, we learned that South Fork was in the middle of a blizzard; it would have been a tough go trying to make it there. It was clear we were meant to stay another day and be there with Cheyanne to celebrate Quinton's thirteenth birthday on December 15.

Cheyanne arrived pretty quickly and was excited that she would have more time with us. We were excited, too, and completely understood that "something" didn't want us on the road this day. We made it to her apartment within a few minutes and settled down to relax, or at least I did. Kristine began to clean and organize Cheyanne's apartment as she cooked a hot meal. Meanwhile, I watched television.

Those who know me know that I'm a "Star Trek: The Next Generation" fan. In *Quinton's Messages,* I told the story of the last episode Quinton and I watched together a short two weeks before he transitioned. In that episode, Data, the android, created his own android daughter who somehow felt emotions. This unprecedented "birth" caught the attention of Star Fleet who wanted to take Data's child for study, but his daughter died before they could take her. It's not a coincidence that this was the last episode Quinton and I watched before he transitioned.

On this particular evening, December 14, 2012, two episodes aired back to back, the last two episodes of their seventh and final season, the 177th and 178th of the Star Trek Next Generation series. The episodes were titled, "All Good Things...," derived from the saying "All Good Things must come to an end." This elongated episode featured Captain Picard's longtime nemesis, Q, who appeared in the very first episode of the series. From my perspective, Q wasn't really a nemesis; he was more of an enlightened being (often annoying) who was in Captain Picard's life to further evolve his way of thinking about the true nature of life and the extra-dimensionality of time.

This episode reminded me of Quinton–our Q and his role in our lives. I believe that Quinton stopped us in our tracks, set me in Cheyanne's family room where I watched this episode, an episode where Captain Picard had to solve a puzzle. The puzzle was to figure out how actions in the present not only affect the future but the past as well. We perceive time as linear, always moving forward, but for extradimensional beings like the Q within this series, it works both ways. I couldn't fathom how the story applied in our reality, but as I sat there watching this final episode of the series, I knew that I was supposed to receive an important message, and that Quinton was there with us.

The next day the icing was applied to the cake, so to speak. Early in the afternoon the Golden Colorado Dodge dealership called to let us know that Q's truck was ready. He said, "I have been in the business for eight years and I have never known a truck to do what your truck did." He went on to say, "the programing on the transmission completely overwrote itself. I have known a mini-van's transmission programming to do this, but never a truck."

Since we knew spirit manipulates electricity quite easily, this was a clear-cut example of Quinton doing so. None of this was a coincidence, and it goes to show that I still have moments where I get it wrong and need significant help to make sound decisions! I recognize it and acknowledge it for what it is.

Chapter Ten

VISITS BY SPIRIT, SHARED BY OTHERS

Quinton's Lesson – *We don't die!*

We found that Quinton's visits with us are not unusual. When we began to share our amazing experiences, others began to tell their own experiences with loved ones visiting from the other side. This is truly where the rubber meets the road when it comes to getting a glimpse of the big picture. It's sad that so many keep these events a secret. While I understand these visits are private and sacred, many don't speak of their visitations out of fear. They worry what others may think or that they may get shut down. They may hear, "Stop that. You don't want people to think you are crazy."

It is truly amazing how "normal" it is for our loved ones to visit us in some shape or form after their transition. The stories you'll read in this chapter are important to illustrate the changing views on this subject; it is becoming more acceptable to share these wondrous events. As we do, more people in our society will accept them. I applaud the courageous individuals who allowed me to share their stories.

Regina Jackson (my sister)

While Kristine and I were living a nightmare, life was going on for those around us. Kristine's recovery from her life-threatening injuries continued to be as miraculous as her wishes circulated through the community; she wanted it known and that we were celebrating Quinton's life. She went so far as to direct those in attendance to wear brightly colored clothing. Meanwhile, I was barely holding on; having been on the go for the first week after the accident, sometimes I was in a daze at times and other times angry.

The service was to be held on June 19, almost nine full days after Quinton's transition. As that day fast approached, those who came to our aid in Farmington had gone back to their lives, but were now returning for the services to be held in Conifer. One of these people was my sister Regina. This is her experience:

It's early in the morning, not sure what time. The sun is streaming in through the open window and the air is crisp for a June morning. Jacque is asleep on the floor, I guess she didn't sleep well either. I wish I could sleep, I wish we didn't have to attend a funeral today. I wish we were here to have fun, to run through the forest, laughing and giggling as we chased each other. I wish, I wish, I wish.... I still can't believe what has happened and we are here for Q's funeral. This is really happening. I fight for sleep wishing the pain would go away. I listen to the birds singing so happily. I think I finally may drift off to sleep.

I am startled. I open my eyes and the room is so bright from the sunlight that I can't see clearly. I look to the floor from the bed and Jacque is sleeping, so sweet and peaceful. I feel like someone else is in the room. I look up and there is Quinton. His face is not clear, but I know it is him. His hair is tasseled and he is wearing shorts and a t-shirt – blue and red (his favorite colors). I will never forget the vibrant red. I am so relieved to see him. It's all been a bad dream, and he has been here the whole time. Something is wrong though, he says, "It's ok, I have to go now." I don't understand, and I tell him he doesn't have to go. I beg him to stay. He insists he must go, but it is ok. It doesn't feel ok. Someone just sucked all the air out of my lungs … it really is happening; he is not going to stay. I think he looks ok, but it is so bright, and I can't see clearly. I want to get up and grab him, but I can't move. Am I awake? Am I asleep? I think I am awake but feel frozen. I can't move – can't make a sound. Quinton is here in this bedroom, and I don't want him to leave. I feel tears on my cheeks … I want to make him stay. He stands by the open window and won't come any closer. I beg him to stay and he tells me no. I want to scream so someone else will come see what I am seeing, but the sound doesn't come out. He tells me, "It will be ok," and then he is gone.

I am up looking for him. He is not there. Ernie is up. I am awake. I was not asleep. He was here. Quinton was here. He's ok; he is not lost in the dark.

It's common to have a deceased loved one tell a survivor, "I have to go now and you can't go with me." Anita Moorjani's book *Dying to Be Me,* illustrates this concept while sharing her near death experience. Her deceased father met with her in heaven while she was deciding whether or not she would return to the physical world. As their conversation progressed he said, "This is as far as you can go, sweetheart. If you go any further, you cannot turn back." (Moorjani, Anita, *Dying to Be Me*, Hay House, Inc., page 74, March 2012.)

***

This story is from a good friend from Colorado I met after Quinton transitioned. She shares the events leading up to the death of her mom and a subsequent visit with her aunt late one evening. It is a blessing when spirit is able to make contact, but it is safe to say, it's especially comforting when unfinished business surrounds the death.

Meghan Pritt

I was lying in the dark, in what was supposed to be the comfort of my basement bedroom, trying to force myself to sleep in preparation of another hard and hopeless day –

much like the two previous weeks. Each day since January 3, 2001, had been relentless and painful since the suspicious disappearance of my best friend–my mother. The mother-child and best friend bonds are powerful. I knew something was terribly wrong the evening before my mom's official disappearance. I was sitting in a chair unwinding and catching up with my stepdad and a family friend when I experienced a sudden onset of anxiety. The attack was random, but even stranger, it was not my anxiety attack. It was very clearly my mother's anxiety, and I was experiencing it on her behalf. I knew something was devastatingly wrong.

My car was in the shop for repair so I asked both my stepdad and his friend to take me to my mom's house five miles down the road because I knew something was wrong. I just had a feeling. They both said I was over-reacting and that everything was fine. Reacting based on a feeling was not something I did. I was known and proud to be one of those people who made decisions based on logic and not emotions. Because I didn't understand the power of intuitions and feelings (and often times made it a point to suppress them), I succumbed to the notion that I was, in fact, over-reacting. However, I still made several phone calls to my mom, all of which went into voicemail. My stepdad, finally unable to ignore my concern and stress, said he would take me to her house in the morning and assured me everything would be fine. I appreciated his acknowledgement of my discontent and offer to help. However, I knew deep down it wasn't going to be okay, but that it was already too late.

My mom and stepdad were undergoing divorce proceedings. My mom stayed in the family house, and my stepdad had purchased a house a few miles down the road. They decided to divorce because they were better business partners than lovers, which was undeniably true. They had run a successful family business together for more than 12 years, but that was all they had done together.

Quinton's Legacy

My stepdad had been in my life from the time I was eight, and we were close. He gave me the love and support that I craved from my father but for some reason never received, despite my efforts to win him over. When I decided to move back to Utah to start my undergraduate degree, I chose to live with my stepdad because my mom had started seeing someone new, and because my stepdad was paying my tuition.

Of course, the decision to live with him over her was equivalent to stabbing my mother in the heart, but my intuition made it clear that I needed to live with my stepdad. I rationalized my feelings with logic and made it known that I was moving in with my stepdad because he was paying my tuition, and that I should live with him to help out with the house as repayment for my education. It was the least I could do. But in all honesty, I moved in with him because I was uncomfortable and skeptical of my mother's new boyfriend of six months. Little did I know my decision to live with my stepdad may have saved my life.

It had been two weeks of frantic searching and convincing the police and news stations that something was undeniably wrong and that my mother would not choose to disappear on her own. All I kept hearing was "adults have the right to disappear," and for that reason we can't help you unless there are obvious signs of foul play. So I began running my own investigation and learned very quickly how to manipulate the police to finally start helping me find my missing mother. My only objective was to find my mother –dead or alive.

The days had been long, emotional and unsuccessful in finding my mother, despite my aggressive efforts, as well as the dedication and determination of friends and family. I had been running on inadequate sleep and food. I learned what true exertion and exhaustion were and, most importantly, I learned how to keep pushing through to try and find my mom.

It was the night before my twenty-first birthday and nearly 10 days since my mom had left the world. I was exhausted, my soul had been beaten down, and I truly felt hopeless. The hopelessness and exhaustion weighed so heavily on my mind and body that I felt like I was slowly, physically being crushed while lying in bed that night. I thought that I might just stop breathing and slip into the unknown. The thought had a strange comfort about it, and I laid there welcoming the possibility. I didn't want to continue to live with the pain and suffering of the unknown, fearing for my life another day.

The last few weeks had brought forth supporting evidence that my mom's boyfriend was, in fact, bad news, and he knew I was after him. I had managed to work with the police to have him put in jail for a parole violation, but I knew his holding would only be temporary and that he would be fueled with anger upon release. I didn't know how long his parole would last, giving me a window of opportunity to rest without fear; but I knew I had at least one night.

The battle between my swirling mind and my body's exhaustion became a force of equal pressure and I became paralyzed in my bed. Shortly after, I felt a presence enter into the stale darkness of my room, shadowed in accompaniment of another. My shallow breathing began to increase and I could feel the instinct to fight pumping through my veins, but I couldn't move or even talk. I laid there in the darkness trying to determine who these two people were, while trying to find a way to break free from my sudden paralyses and escape. One person kept in the shadows in the corner of my room, and the other person paced with angst and frustration back-and-forth at the foot of my bed. The urge to fight quickly dissipated when I realized it was my mother and the aunt I never knew due to her passing from Lupus before I was born. They were standing in the dark of my room.

The atmosphere filled with a sense of relief, peace and awkwardness. My mother had fought the confines between death and earth to see me one last time. There were no audible words exchanged between us, but the message was clear. She was there to apologize. She was clearly devastated by her unexpected departure from earth and disgusted with herself for not seeing the obvious signs of a bad relationship, and for not taking my advice to sever her relationship with her boyfriend. But most of all, she was sorry for leaving me alone in the world and not being there to protect me. It was obvious that she had been festering with frantic mother's guilt for prematurely departing the world, and she felt her death was her own fault even though it was at the hand of another.

I calmly told her what had happened was not her fault and reassured her that I was going to be fine; nor was I angry with her for what happened and the burden she left me to bear. I told her it was time to forgive herself, step into the next phase of her life without guilt and to find true happiness. My message then released her spirit and she was able to step into the next dimension of her life seeking peace and happiness with my aunt. And that was the last time I saw my mom.

***

In 2012, as I flitted around telling about our journey with anyone interested, many shared their own experiences with me. The following was written by Michelle Tanner, fellow property manager in Denver who told me her story over lunch after a presentation. It was so interesting, I asked if I could include it in my book. She shares multiple experiences that she and her family members have had:

Michelle Tanner

Let me start by saying that my first experience with people in my life to make their transition started way back when I was about 10 years old. This is really my mom's experience, but the possibility that there is something more than this physical presence we all know. My mother was pregnant with my sister Renee in 1979. In January of that year, my grandpa passed away and then three months later my grandma, who helped me to be open, passed away in our home. Later that year, in September, my mother gave birth to my sister Renee. While this has no bearing on the story, I believe my mother's senses were heightened due to the pregnancy, possibly opening her up to sense things she might not have otherwise.

Many strange things happened in that house after my maternal grandmother died. My mother woke up to find both of her parents standing at the foot of her bed. These were full-color figures, no mistaking who was there, just standing at the foot of the bed watching her sleep. That was the first sign of them. My grandmother died in the bathroom of our home, and needless to say, she played havoc with the toilet in that bathroom. The water would run often and when my mom would yell at her to stop, the water would instantly stop running. I witnessed that myself when I was 10 years old.

As I grew older and lost other people in my life, I experienced more sightings, feelings, dreams and touches. In high school, a friend of mine named Xavier passed away during our senior year in a tragic car accident. This was a hard pill to swallow in high school, losing someone so young for no obvious reason. Wrong place at the wrong time, I suppose; or at least that's how I rationalized it.

I started dating his brother later during my senior year and spent a lot of time at the house with Xavier's family. My boyfriend moved into Xavier's room, and that is where I saw him. I saw a misty silhouette of a person in the dark. I thought it was my imagination as I lay there in the dark, all alone. But I closed my eyes and opened them again, and he was still there. I closed my eyes again, just to make sure this was not my imagination, and again the silhouette was still there. There was no question in my mind that Xavier was standing in the doorway of his bedroom.

My paternal grandpa Hales passed away in September of 2000 in Florida, where he and my grandma had moved from Colorado. I decided to go visit my grandma in Florida a couple years later. Grams was still very uneasy and didn't sleep well. As a matter of fact, she slept on the couch because she was up and down so much. She offered me her bedroom, since she didn't sleep in there anyway. One night, and if I remember correctly, it was the third night I was there, I snuggled into bed and turned on my side with my back to the door. The house was comfortable with the central air, actually a bit cool, so I got up under the covers. I laid there with my eyes closed, trying to get my brain to shut down from the day's activities. All of a sudden, I felt this warm sensation, almost like someone running their hands down my side and back, and I was feeling the heat from their hands. I can't be 100 percent sure, but I would guess that was a sign from my grandpa. Warm hugs from heaven perhaps.

My latest encounter was a dream I had in October of 2011, the 10-year anniversary of my father's death. My dad, who died in October 2001 at the young age of 48, appeared in my dream. I don't dream of him often or get signs from him often, but there was no mistaking who was there in my dream. Before I tell you of this dream, I have to paint a picture of a man who was a free spirit, did what he wanted, when he wanted and never met a stranger. He could charm a snake, if he could get that close. He was a man who didn't need a lot of material things; he lived his life with necessities and didn't much care for some fashion police telling him what to wear. So with that said, he appeared to me in my dream wearing a pair of boxer shorts and cowboy boots. That's it, looking in a full-sized mirror telling his reflection how handsome he was. That was my dad. What a goof he was. That dream was something I will never forget because I woke up literally smiling. As I write this, I find myself smiling again!

My experiences haven't been of great magnitude, but the point is that I've had them, and I've been open enough to receive them. I'm one of the lucky ones who have had a chance to experience my loved ones' presence once they have crossed over. Those memories are something I can keep with me forever!

Michelle's experiences *have* been of great magnitude; remember, we can't compare our losses and visits with others. They are divine and essentially for us. The memory of loved ones making contact after they have transitioned to pure energy does stay with us forever. More than that, they change us for the better; that "Divine and Awful Dichotomy." When we have these experiences, even though we desperately miss our departed loved ones, we can't help but know there is more; know that they still exist. This realization changes the way we see the world we live in. How could it not?

***

The story below is from a classmate, Pete Stuhr, from the graduating class of 1983 at Evergreen High School. He shares contacts made by two of his brothers after they died, one of which not only saved his life but the lives of three of his friends.

Pete Stuhr

First, thank you for writing and sharing *Quinton's Messages*! I just finished reading it, and I am inspired to e-mail you. I feel I have a few things to share with you.

Your book gave me chills at times, and I got to share two of my experiences of loved one's passing on. Although I believe a loved one moves on to a higher plane after making sure the ones here on earth are ok, they can come back . . . .

94

Quinton's Legacy

It was sometime in the late 80s. Four friends and I decided to drive back to Colorado from Tempe/ASU in my friend's Camaro. Being quite tall, I decided the way to be most comfortable was to drive. We departed in the evening, and it was well into the night when we approached an area of two-lane highway that was dead straight for a long time, right before it made two 90-degree bends to cross a canyon. I fell asleep while driving the straight away (no alcohol or drugs). I distinctly remember my brother Robbie (who passed on in a 1969 plane crash) nudging me awake in time to make the first 90-degree bend, but just barely. I think he increased my heart rate so much I could drive on for a while!

Another brother of mine, Chip (I'm the youngest of nine) "transitioned" as you like to say, a few years ago from lung cancer. On the day he died, I was playing golf early in the morning at Wingpointe golf course in Salt Lake City. I was playing alone and walking the course, as I love to do. I was playing pretty well. I was surprised to miss the seventeenth green. I hit a good chip, and it went into the hole! I missed the eighteenth green as well, and then hit a horribly bad chip that was careening across the green sure to find the bunker, or worse, when it hit the pin and dropped in! I could only laugh, and then I realized I felt Chip's presence! I got home, and my dad had left a message that Chip had died.

We are truly inspired and amazed at how God works! I imagine some readers may not understand how we speak of spirit communication, psychics, mediums and God in the same sentence. But truly, God is the one who makes it all possible. All of it goes hand in hand; it is mutually inclusive, not exclusive. Our intention in sharing our experiences is to assist others with their grief and their healing.

***

The story below is from a young lady who was struggling with the death of her father. She sent a text message to my wife after reading *Quinton's Messages*.

Mia

> Hi Kristine,
>
> This is Mia (TK's friend). I just wanted to share with you a moment I had this morning. I was sitting on the couch reading the end of *Quinton's Messages*, feeling a little discouraged as I still had not encountered any messages of my own (Mia's father transitioned February 12, 2011), and then it happened. It has been so hot in my apartment at night that I had a fan in the windowsill. I turned it off before bed, and then all of a sudden it turned on for about five seconds and then shut off again. I even got up to check, and it was definitely off! I felt so connected to the other side; I wanted to share with you and Ernie! Thank you for opening my eyes!

Mia makes a very good point. To feel connected to our departed loved ones makes a difference in the grieving process; it certainly helps with the sadness and loss. Wouldn't it be wonderful if we could hold on to that momentary elation forever?

***

I heard the next amazing story when I was working at Prime West. I met Judy, who worked directly for the owner of the three buildings that I managed. Finally the day came where I had the pleasure of meeting her in person when she came into town. We arrived at a luncheon set-up to recognize the entire development team responsible for completing 385 Interlocken almost a year prior. I was introduced to Judy, and during lunch–when I shared my experiences–she told me that her mom had transitioned just a few weeks earlier. This is what she shared with me:

Judith Waugh

In the spring of 2011, Judith Waugh's mom was dying after a valiant fight with throat cancer. Judy and her brother were with her one day in her hospital room as death approached. She was in and out of consciousness during the day while both of her grown children were spending time with her. On that particular day, her mom became more alert and started speaking to someone at the foot of the bed. She was talking to *her mother*, Judy and her brother's deceased grandmother. Judy had to shush her brother as he started wondering out loud why his mom was talking to imaginary people. Judy had the presence of mind to know that she really was talking to her deceased mother!

It happens all too often and has been shared by numerous people, in numerous books, what a special privilege it is to be present physically prior to a loved one's transition. Many times, when the individual is close to transitioning, they begin to communicate with a loved one who is on the other side. Perhaps the veil between worlds lifts and the loved ones can be sensed and are ready to accompany them home. Whether we believe this is possible or not, keep an open mind. The next story is another example.

Andy Seitz and his wife

I met Andy in 1991 while working for my father's janitorial company. We were close during the decade of the 90s and quickly went from being clients to friends. Sometimes I get tapped on the shoulder to make a difference in the life of another, and so I feel I was called to be there for Andy during one of his toughest challenges. During the 90s, we spent a lot of time together going to see his boys play football for the Mountain View Toros. Since then we've stayed in contact, sporadically, after 1998 and then reconnected after *Quinton's Messages* had been published.

Andy is a devout Mormon and very involved in the church. He talks the talk, but more so, he walks the walk. During one of our visits to Phoenix in 2012, we met for lunch. We talked about our journey and he shared his thoughts about my first book. I am always a little nervous when I speak about our experiences with our religious friends. I just don't know how they will receive what I have to share. While Andy didn't agree with all of what was written, I later learned (via a book, *Life Everlasting* by Duane S. Crowther) many members of the Mormon faith embrace near death experiences and believe that we exist beyond "death." During our visit, he shared the following story:

Andy's wife's sister transitioned just before our meeting. She and her partner were atheists, believing adamantly that once you died, everything faded to black. They thought that at death, they faded into nothingness. With this in mind, Andy's sister-in-law fought to stay alive, but soon it became clear that that fading to nothingness was not going to happen. Andy and his wife spent a lot of time with the couple in the hospital as death approached. While her partner was distraught, Andy spent time preparing his sister-in-law for death by telling her not to be surprised at what was to come, even though it's difficult to explain this mystical experience.

As the days went on, she began to see visions of those she loved who had preceded her in the great beyond–they were in the room with her. She began to point and gesture, even talking with them while Andy assured her that it was okay. "What you are seeing is real." Her partner didn't believe any of it; she thought the pain medicine was causing her to hallucinate.

***

These last two stories above are the norm; they are commonplace. It is quite common for a person who is near death, incoherent or unconscious to suddenly become lucid, staring at someone in the room that nobody else can see. They converse with that unseen person, calling them mom, or dad or grandmother. As I've said before, there are no rules; this is a frequent occurrence.

***

Bob Pieper

If you read *Quinton's Messages,* you'll remember Bob Pieper, who was directly responsible for transporting my family and me back to Conifer after Quinton transitioned. Brother Bob is what I call this mountain of a man who stands 6'5" tall and is a muscular, 270-pounds. He played football at Evergreen High School and, subsequently, for the University of Kansas.

In 2011, Bob was working in Australia but came back to visit his dad, who was very ill, as much as he could. During the holidays in 2011, his dad's condition worsened. Bob knew he may never see him again, but he needed to go back to work. Six weeks later he received the call that he had hoped wouldn't come. His dad was in the hospital and fading quickly. Bob hopped on the next available flight. As Bob tells it, "The flight over the Pacific Ocean is always calm; I've never encountered any turbulence, but this flight was different."

While Bob flew over the Pacific, his dad's doctors were working to keep their patient alive a little longer. They put him on life support while Bob's brother and family watched, anguished over the startling and sudden turn of events. Bob's dad, not unlike Bob himself, was a mountain of a man, and no one wanted to see him suffer any more. After one hour and 40 minutes, Bob's brother made the decision to remove life support, and he quietly passed over to the other side. Meanwhile, Bob's flight had an unexpected development – serious turbulence.

As Bob tells it, this turbulence "caught everyone off guard – even the pilots. Our plane was violently tossed; everyone had their seat belts on, even the flight attendants. Personal effects were flying around as people started getting motion sickness. We all hung on for dear life. This lasted one hour and 40 minutes!" Bob flies a lot, but he had never seen anything like this before in severity and duration. It gets more interesting.

Upon eventually arriving in Denver and taking care of all the arrangements with his family for his father's services and burial, he learned more of the details of his father's life support. Bob is an engineer and keenly tuned into details. So the one hour and 40 minutes of turbulence and one hour and 40 minutes his father spent on life support, and the time the turbulence occurred, coincided exactly after accounting for the time zone difference.

What are the odds of this happening? The odds are simply just too high to try explaining this away to a simple coincidence!

Jeannie and David Bernard

Being president of Building Owners and Managers Association (BOMA) in Denver is a three-year term: the first year as president elect, then a year as the president and the last year as immediate past president. The association is a volunteer organization with approximately 350 members made up of property managers (principal members) and service providers (allied members). Both principal and allied members tend to be very busy as they attempt to keep up with their respective job requirements. This applies to the officers of the chapters, too. We could not effectively manage our chapter without a strong executive vice president like Jeannie Bernard.

I relied on Jeannie and worked closely with her. Given our working relationship, her husband David and my wife Kristine were also close.

The truth be told, that friendship began long before, but was cemented, as they were part of our journey when Quinton transitioned. Often when we weren't talking about BOMA, we would have conversations more spiritual in nature, including their amazing experiences.

Jeannie's dad Vito (Mack was his nickname) was a master electrician and a prankster with a sense of humor. Jeannie's husband David had a special relationship with him as both David and Jeannie's dad were veterans. David was a medic in Vietnam, and Jeannie's dad Vito fought in Burma during World War II. These two gentlemen lived the horrors of war and could discuss the horrific experiences each had with one another, knowing the other would understand.

Alma, Jeannie's sister-in-law, succumbed to a long battle with cancer and the day of her funeral, sadly, Jeannie's dad died. Jeannie pulled out the stops to make it back to Maryland in time for the services. She arrived late but had time to see her dad and say hello. The next day he woke and was bumping into walls as he walked. When she found out he had been doing that for a couple of days, she surmised he had had a stroke and immediately had him admitted to the hospital for treatment.

Vito knew he had cancer but stated that he would not go through chemotherapy as Alma had done. On the way back from Alma's funeral, Jeannie got the call that he had died.

That night after Alma's service and after Vito died, Jeanne stayed with her sister, Gloria. As they sat around reminiscing about their dad, one light began to flicker. It was the lamp in the room they were in. There were other lights on in the house, but this particular light was the only one flickering. They turned it off, checked the bulb, cord and plug. Everything was in order, but the lamp kept flickering when they turned it back on. Jeannie knew that it was her dad!

This instance that Jeannie shares is very common. Spirit is adept at manipulating electricity (source: Van Praagh, James, *Growing up in Heaven*, page 142), and given that he was a master electrician, they knew it was her dad. Interestingly, Jeannie didn't think of death in terms of being able to make contact after death. But this event was so profound and unusual that she quickly put two and two together and knew it was her dad. It gets even better!

When Jeannie and David received her dad's Oldsmobile after he transitioned, they took it to the shop to have everything checked out and then started driving it. But a funny thing started happening when they drove it; the fuel gauge started acting very odd. When the tank was full, the gauge would show it empty and vice-versa. It was like the gauge had a mind of its own. They actually went so far as to take it to the shop and have it replaced, but the new gauge did the same thing! Finally, they could not take this particular shenanigan anymore. The car was wonderful, and they loved driving it, but they really did need to know how much gas was in the tank. One day they looked heavenward and spoke to dear old dad. They politely asked him to knock it off, and the "problem" stopped shortly thereafter, never to return.

These next two stories of how Vito demonstrated his presence had me laughing with Jeannie and David.

Once, as they stood in line ordering food, something got them to thinking about dear old dad. As they waited they got their drinks and left them on the table they had chosen. They continued talking about him as they went back to get their food. Suddenly, six feet away, with nobody around, Jeannie's Coke flew off their table! They knew Vito was messing with them, as there weren't any other explanations.

They had one more story of Vito. David and one of their grandchildren had gone to the grocery store and as they were going down an aisle, stuff started flying off the shelves. There was nobody around! A can or box of produce would suddenly catapult into the middle of the aisle. This happened several times and, of course, they knew it was Vito – ever the prankster!

***

This next segment, although short, covers three common themes. First, sometimes our loved ones who are transitioning see those who have preceded them to the other side of the veil. Second, spirit often manipulates electricity to get our attention when visiting. Third, sometimes children have an easier time sensing Spirit.

Marty Jones

Here is my story:

> My grandmother raised 15 kids on the farm. I have a huge family, immediate and extended with cousins whom I was just meeting for the first time. My grandmother was dying, and there were only a few who were able to say goodbye to her. The family members said that the moment right before her passing, she had her hand out and said that grandpa was right there holding her hand. Shortly afterward, she passed on her own.
>
> That night something special happened. My son Andrew was 10 months old at the time. My wife woke up in the middle of the night and heard my son laughing. She went over to the crib and saw his shoes lighting up and a toy light coming on. My wife felt the presence of my grandmother and said to her, "Grandmother, thank you for visiting, but let Andrew sleep now." Once she said that, the shoe and his toy stopped lighting up. When my dad came to visit with us, we discussed with him what had happened. When I was telling the story, Andrew's toy, which was in the middle of the room, started to light up again!

The funeral was amazing. All the family members were talking about their personal experiences of grandma visiting. It seems the grandkids got most of the visits. One particular grandchild said that grandma came down from the ceiling and said good-bye. Every family member had some kind of an experience with grandma.

Kristine and I continue to be blessed by those we have met during our journey. Yet another dichotomy is that the subject of death is the catalyst for the meeting. Vickie Baroch falls into that category. Not long after her fiancé passed away, we met at Wystone's Tea House, located within the Belmar retail area. We were unable to recognize her when she walked up because she was so somber. I mention this only to remind you that, yes, at times we are somber; it is a heavy burden we carry. However, after I took a chance and hailed her, that smile and twinkle in her eyes that her fiancé fell in love with arrived with force. It was then we met Vickie.

Below is Vickie's story of how she met Walt Whitney, how they fell in love, the story of his passing, and subsequently how he let her know that he is still there for her. You can feel her pain; we can relate to her pain. But through this pain came the knowledge that there is no death.

Vickie Baroch-The Touch of a Kind Soul

Angels on Earth exist. If it wasn't divine intervention, it may have been that Walt and I were not blessed with the time we had on this earth together.

After random meetings in passing at the pool of our apartments and a few conversations in the parking lot, finally, around the first part of October, Walt asked me if I would like to have dinner with him. I was thrilled, and we went to Siena in Castle Rock. It was a busy week, as I was deep in the midst of preparations for events at my office, and then headed to Seattle to visit friends as soon as the week's duties were complete. Looking back on how special that night was, it seemed that all those things took a back seat to a connection that neither Walt nor I were aware at that time would run so deep. Or, as I now know, heartfelt, blessed and filled with serendipitous love connections.

We talked, laughed and got to know each other. Walt told me later in our short life together that was the night he really fell in love with me. He loved to (in his words) "watch my eyes dance when you talk and laugh." It was a lovely time and forever cherished in my heart.

I had one more night before I flew to Seattle. On that evening, Walt had asked if I wanted to get a bite to eat, which I most certainly did, WITH HIM. Then he offered to take some of the pressure off my schedule and help me pack to get ready by bringing dinner over. This gentleman of mine "had me at hello" (as the movie lore goes). He showed up with a bottle of wine, two wine glasses in hand and a cooler with some dinner takeout, so I wouldn't have to worry about any dishes that night. We talked for a long while that night over dinner. When he left he took the garbage from my apartment out for me and also took my luggage down to the car for me. Then, as we said goodnight and how fun it would be to keep in touch on the road (he had a trip coming up that would keep him traveling for a week after I returned), he was so very sweet in asking if he might kiss me. What do you think I said?

After he got back from traveling, he told me there were things in place for him to actually be moving away from Colorado, but he wanted to spend as much time with me as possible until then. But, again, divine timing and intervention–he stayed . . . stayed and still stayed . . . then stayed for good here in Colorado. He stayed here for me and for us. We were so happy! In our time together, we enjoyed beginning a life together that would be truly a gift.

Walt left on a Monday night, April 22, 2013 (Earth Day). He had not been feeling good for a few days before then but seemed to be on the mend. I came home from work a little early, as we were getting snow that night and I wanted to be with him. We were dog sitting in Bell Mountain, and I also wanted to get home before driving on the roads became more difficult.

We enjoyed being together that night as every night. At one point, I asked if he wanted to lie down in the bedroom. I wondered if he would be more comfortable there—where I could bring him a blanket. He said, "No, I want to be right where I am, here with you," and we continued to talk, laugh, watch movies and hang out with the dogs together. At one point, we sat together and hugged. I told him he was going to be feeling better; that our friend Ray had told me that the biggest support system for him was me being there. I told Walt, "I love you, you are getting better and I am not going anywhere." He hugged me back, and said as well, "I love YOU and I am not going anywhere."

Around 9:15 that evening, after being so sweet as he always was, taking the dogs out to the backyard, Walt was gone from me. He had a water bottle in his hand, which I heard crunch. He was within a foot of me on the couch. He fell over to one side, toward me and facing toward the floor, without a sound or a final word.

After the medics arrived, my heart will never forget the gentle fireman who was the one to come over to me and with compassion and kindness, say that they had tried everything but Walt was not able to be revived. **What I do know for sure is this: he was with me and exactly where he wanted to be. He was loved, he adored and loved me. He was happy and at peace**!

In the minutes, hours, days and months since, life has taken on a hue and a surreal sense that I cannot explain beyond the grief of losing (and now on a journey to recovering) my heart and soul. We had been through so much together in such a short amount of time. We had just become engaged officially on Valentine's Day, although we had talked about it in advance and told family and close friends. Walt even asked my parents for their permission to marry me, which touched them deeply as they knew how happy I was. On Valentine's night at dinner, Walt asked me to marry him with these words: "I love you, Sweetie. I adore you, and I want to spend the rest of my life with you." And indeed, he did exactly that.

Since his transition, there have been things that have shown up that I trust will eventually renew that faith in things "unseen" and "beyond the veil." The separation between *here* and *there* is, as a kind friend and pastor at Walt's funeral service described, no real difference between *here* and *there*. *There* is just *here* without the *T*."

How do I know there is a realm that is beyond the veil? How do I *know* Walt is still here for me? These are the glimpses I see:

A "knowing" in my heart and soul of a love that Walt and I share. An entire lifetime condensed into a time on this earth that was far too short . . . but a connection that runs far deeper than time on a calendar.

The blue jay that showed up at my brother's office window within a day of Walt's church service. Never before had a bird showed up at the window of the office, literally pecking against the window, time after time, as if to say, "Hey you – I am here!" He would land on the tree outside the office, then take flight over to the window with barely a ledge to stand upon, peck at the window a few times and fly back to the tree. Over and over, and for many days after Walt's passing this is what the blue jay did.

In the clouds where I looked up one day the summer after Walt transitioned to see a huge "W" in the puffy white clouds of a beautiful blue sky.

In a Christmas gift from friends. A journal containing pictures of birds and dragonflies with a saying special to me for the connection through the birds to the sky: "I pray to the birds because I believe they will carry the messages of my heart upward," by Terry Tempest Williams.

In what I call "fur fixes" where beautiful dogs make their way to me. I feel comfort and sense they may be comforting me and Walt, or perhaps on behalf of Walt at the same time (he loved dogs, as do I!). One day while at breakfast with friends in Castle Pines, within a few weeks after Walt passed, neighbors of my friends met us there and they happened to have several of their dogs with them. I couldn't hold myself back from going to pet them because they were beautiful, and Walt would have loved them. They came over to me immediately with the unconditional love dogs hold for all of us! Those loving dogs, took me out of my sadness for at least a few moments.

At Walt's service, which was attended by an overflowing church of attendees, I pulled all of the courage I had together and read this:

The Adventure of life is to Learn.
The Goal of life is to Grow.
The Nature of life is to Change.
The Challenge of life is to Overcome.
The Essence of life is to Care.
The Secret of life is to Dare.
The Beauty of life is to Give.
The Joy of life is to Love.
by William Arthur Ward (1921-1994)
Walt loved me and I loved him. He was my "Joy of Life."
A gift beyond measure.

In the spring of 2014, I finally broke down and utilized a Phoenix-based dentist. It seems that I can be rather stubborn, going to my dentist in Conifer, Colorado whenever I was back in Colorado instead of finding a dentist in Arizona. I no longer tell so many people about Quinton's visits, but during this first visit to an Arizona dentist, I found myself sharing with the hygienist. Her eyes grew wide: "You have to talk with Sharan!" After the x-rays, cleaning, and meeting with the dentist, I met Sharan who also worked at the office. She has the most beautiful energy; something about her is very bright and open. She has been sensing Spirit since she was a child; her ability to sense her departed loved ones has not left her. This is what she shared with me:

Sharan Lambert

My first recollection was when I was three years old. My maternal grandfather passed away at my parents' home in Tucson. My grandparents had been visiting from Virginia and, unfortunately, he had a heart attack. We had to drive to Virginia for the funeral. On the way there my grandfather sang to us in the car. My mother, father, and grandmother were all present when we heard him singing "Sweet Chariot." A deep baritone voice singing, "Swing low, sweet chariot . . . ." I can still remember the shocked look on everyone's face and the wonder if we all heard his voice.

The second occurrence was eight or nine years after my maternal grandmother passed. She had never met my children, as they had not been born when she was alive. I had a realistic dream where she was sitting quite content in a cottage welcoming my two children and me into her home. We sat in the kitchen, and she fixed us food and then thanked me for letting her meet her great grandchildren. As we left the house and she walked us to the picket fence, I asked her if she was coming with us. She answered, "No dear, this is as far as I can come. I just wanted to meet the children." I woke up still feeling as though she was in the room.

Now I'll tell about the more painful of my recollections. My son Keith was 24 years old when he died. How he died doesn't matter much now after nine years; it is better to let that go. However, I'll share the things that happened after he died. The realistic dreams started about three days after he passed. It was almost like he was purging the things he had done in this life. Some of it was very graphic and painful. I think I had to see this so I could understand that he was sorry. Here is one of the positive dreams that turned out to be a premonition:

He was a little boy riding in a truck with me, and he grabbed my hand and said, "Don't forget to get the keychain!" We pulled up in front of a house and an older man with thinning hair came out; he almost reached us when I woke up. I told this to my husband when I woke up because I felt the need for a witness, but I really didn't understand why. On the day of Keith's funeral, a man with thinning hair approached me and told me what a wonderful person Keith was and they wouldn't have eaten on some days without him. He then handed me a keychain with a fish on it. That keychain had been with him in Vietnam. He carried it with him and now he wanted me to have it. I got goose bumps when that happened.

Also, on the day of his funeral, we suddenly had hundreds of flies inside the house on the window in the kitchen. I couldn't believe they weren't flying around. I could have scooped them up, but instead I just opened the window and they all flew out.

My husband (not Keith's father) also had a realistic dream where the song "Dream Weaver" was playing in his mind. That night he felt the bed move and he jumped out and asked if I felt that. I said no and started laughing, thinking that was exactly something my mischievous son would do!

Quinton's Legacy

From that time on after, "Dream Weaver" was impressed on us, and my son would visit me in my dreams. He would come in the morning before I woke so I could "feel" his hugs and understand things were okay. He stayed with me on and off for five years. I haven't had any dreams about him for a long time, but I know if I need him, he will give me a nudge in my dreams.

Chapter Eleven

GEHRIG DONALD KILBURN

Quinton's Lesson: Spirit can make contact any number of ways!

Mark Kilburn is a friend of mine. He is an author of poetry, newspaper columns and a book titled *Last Song: A True Lakota Love Story* I love so much that I wrote a review for it on Amazon. Our bond grew closer still as he helped edit this manuscript. During a dinner meeting in Aurora at Sam's #3 Restaurant on July 18, 2014, he shared some of his son Gehrig's exploits as spirit, which are so impactful that they make up their own chapter.

Given the fact that Mark is an author himself, he wrote a very touching chapter. Don't be surprised if you are moved to tears of joy and appreciation for the many ways in which Gehrig was able to make his presence known.

For so many of us, meeting Ernie Jackson can be the direct result of the worst possible fate humans can possibly endure, the loss of a child. For me it was the last week of April 2012 when my son Gehrig Donald Kilburn, just 23 years old, was killed by a drugged and drunken, unlicensed, hit and run driver.

The same Heidi Saltzman that Ernie talks about in both his first and second books happened to also be my grief counselor. She gave me both the book *Quinton's Messages*, and the author, Ernie Jackson's phone number, urging me to call him. I read the book that first week after my son's death and also called Ernie, meeting an advocate and someone I hoped would be a lifelong friend. Dazed, defeated and depressed, it was Ernie who patiently listened and guided me through this life-altering tragedy and worst case scenario. The book was such a help I eventually read it twice.

Ernie was like the big brother I never had and one of the very few people I felt could understand this terrible journey I'd been forced to take. Grief counselors refer to cases like mine and Ernie's as complicated grief, due to the fact that there is a lengthy trial involved after the funeral. This trial hell was yet another part of the difficult process that Ernie had already endured and could counsel and prepare me for, continually offering me his support while forewarning me of the messages that had either occurred or were about to occur.

In the first week after my son's death, I'd gone to the store. When I got out of my car, I saw some change lying on the ground. I said to myself, 'pennies from heaven,' and scooped it up, counting 37 cents. When I mentioned this to my ex-wife she told me how threes and sevens kept popping up throughout Gehrig's life as well as after his passing, and that they were his two favorite numbers. I put the change in a jar on my desk and didn't give it a lot of thought after that.

A couple months later I was feeling sorry for myself because it seemed everyone in Gehrig's family was having dreams about him except me. I remembered the 37 cents but selfishly wanted more from my son. Again I went to the store, parking in the same row; when I opened the car door I immediately saw 27 cents lying by my car. My first thought was that this couldn't be from Gehrig since it wasn't 37 cents, and I walked toward the store. As I passed the next car, there shining in the sun laid a brand new dime, minted in Denver, and I knew. I knew without a doubt that this was how my son chose to communicate with me and that he was still here, trying to ease the pain caused by his passing. More than two years have gone by since finding 37 cents twice within just a few weeks after his passing, and I haven't found more than a few pennies and one dime since then, which just cements the fact that it was a sign from my son, in my mind anyway. I keep the 74 (37 x 2) cents on my desk.

My little story is pretty insignificant compared to some of the experiences other people have had, both friends and family. I am just now finding out exactly how many people close to my son have received "messages" from him. Although it's been a bittersweet task, I've collected some of the most poignant and touching experiences. I must start with the most intense of the group, which happened to my niece, Jillian.

Jillian, Gehrig's cousin

Jill was one of Gehrig's many cousins, and green is her favorite color; just like Gehrig. One day she picked out a bright green t-shirt to wear to work and, like always, it made her think of her lost cousin. All the cousins were and are very close, more like brothers and sisters than typical cousins. Green would prove to be a most fortuitous choice and perhaps even helped to save her life since it made her think of Gehrig (we still call him "G"). He was forefront on her mind as she headed off to work.

Jill had been working for several months at a halfway house in the summer of 2013, barely a year after G's passing, when one of the ex-cons decided to get his hands on an assault rifle and commit mass murder. He entered the halfway house armed with a fully loaded AR-15 (30 round clip), and because Jill was working the front desk, she was his first victim.

She tells how the gun was aimed directly between her eyes and that when the felon pulled the trigger, he should have blown her head off.

Indeed, she recalled waiting for her skull to explode. The Plexiglas shattered when he fired, and that made her wince and blink. Somehow, despite the fact that he was only a couple feet away, the shot inexplicably missed. Jill dove for cover, lying on the floor under her desk.

Then the gunman took aim and shot her co-worker, Chris, who was trying to crawl away toward the back offices. The gunman shot and hit him. Jill recalls that the gunman was firing madly the entire time. After he shot her co-worker, he began to back away toward the front door, still firing at will toward Jill. And he was obviously trying to cause murder and mayhem. When he began firing, Jill said it was instant insanity, chaotic and extremely loud, confusing and difficult to recall. Even though she saw the entire thing, her brain kept telling her it was just fireworks; this is how insane, crazy, and sudden this attack was. It seemed her brain had a difficult time accepting what it saw.

Jill was most likely in shock or close to it, running only on instinct, adrenalin and her will to live. Under the Plexiglas window, there was only a single sheet of ultra-thin paneling, unbelievably the three shots that hit the thin paneling actually altered course and ricocheted away from Jill for some reason that defied physics. Had they not altered course, all three would have hit Jill in her back! It appears that she'd experienced another miracle each time the shooter pulled the trigger, making for multiple miracles that night.

The maniacal gunman backed up through the front door and ran away, leaving total chaos in his wake; Jill remained under her desk until hearing voices as the groggy inmates left their rooms to see what was happening. Jill was forced to deal with the 120 inmates, call 9-1-1, and all the while coping with her wounded co-worker Chris. He was shot, and although not a life-threatening injury, it was serious enough to be grotesque. Chris had obviously slipped into shock as well, and Jill had to get him calmed and sitting down, as he kept trying to stand up. By the time she accomplished this, the police finally arrived.

It was then Jill was allowed to think, and when she did, she thought of Gehrig. In fact, Gehrig was all she thought of for the next hour. Jill could hear his voice inside of her head repeating, "I got your back Jill. I got your back!"

She was aware of his presence ever since she'd donned the bright green t-shirt earlier in the day, and he'd been on her mind, but that was nothing compared to the intense feelings she now experienced. When she first sat down, her head was flooded with crazy, racing thoughts. These random, wild, chaotic thoughts swept through her head and she was all over the map until she thought of Gehrig. Once she thought of her cousin, all that craziness inside her brain immediately and permanently ended; she felt a serene calmness come over her as he made his presence felt. She heard his voice reassuring her and she knew without doubt at that point that Gehrig had protected and saved her life. Although she never saw him, either in dream or vision, she was 100 percent sure he was with her and had saved at least two lives that night.

A sergeant talked with Jill afterward and agreed that Jill had been a very lucky girl, that it wasn't her time yet, and that she certainly had someone watching over her. She said, "You sure got that right!"

"I got your back Jilly!" were the words G kept repeating as she sat by herself for that entire hour, totally wrapped up in thoughts of Gehrig and gratitude for how lucky she was to be alive. Jill knew Gehrig had saved her and her friend's life that night, and she was and is very grateful. She finished talking to me with this little nugget. "Gehrig had a really strong and powerful personality. Now I know his spirit is every bit as strong, if not stronger!"

What I know is that it's pretty much impossible for even the worst and poorest of all shooters to miss any stationary target four times in a row when that target is lying motionless and at point blank range. There had to be some sort of intervention from somewhere or something for my niece to be with us today. I doubt my family could have withstood a second tragedy of this magnitude so to me it makes perfect sense that my son saved all of us further shock and pain by saving Jilly. But there have been many more sightings, visits, whatever you want to call them.

Zerell Worely, Gehrig's Best Friend from First Grade until Now

Green was Gehrig's favorite color, and seven was his favorite number. Throughout the messages various friends and family have received from G., both the color and number continually pop up.

Gehrig's best friend from first grade until death was a wonderful young man named Zerell Worley. Zerell became a father for the first time in early 2014 when he and his wife gave birth to Ares Gehrig Worley; Gehrig would have made a great uncle and godfather, but it was not meant to be. Because Zerell and Gehrig were so close for so many years, his death has been awfully tough for Zerell. Like all of us, he continues to struggle with the loss.

On a particularly tough day, Zerell was driving with Ares when Ares began screaming. Earlier in the day Zerell had gotten that phone call we all dread; his boss informed him that he'd been laid off. So now he had a brand new baby, gets this terrible news that he's laid off, and his son is suddenly screaming louder and louder while poor Zerell is ready to have a nervous breakdown. In fact, he admitted to me that he was on the verge of tears when he looked up and saw Gehrig's sign.

In Colorado, the highway department puts up signs on the roadsides for people killed on the highway: In Memory of John Doe – Please Drive Safely! Gehrig's sign is on the exit of Federal and Colfax Avenue, on the onramp leading from west bound Colfax to southbound Federal, not far from where Zerell lives. Zerell spoke to Gehrig, saying "G, I wish you were here so you could take my son for a few hours. You were always there for me, and I could always count on you."

Right at that exact moment, Zerell drove by the sign, pulled over and got a bottle out for his son who was screaming louder and louder every second. But as soon as he stopped, his boy quit screaming and grew all wide-eyed and quiet while staring at the sky above and behind them.

Zerell turned, looked up, and saw what he described as a perfect seven that the only cloud in the sky had magically formed. Suddenly Ares fell silent and within seconds had fallen into a deep and peaceful sleep. All of a sudden it seemed as if the storm in his life had passed and calm returned. But wait, as if this isn't enough, there is even more! Zerell's phone rang right then before he started driving. It was a call from someplace he'd applied for a job several months prior and had never heard back from. They now had an immediate opening if he still wanted the job.

This was no dream; this was the unbreakable bond that only best friends, nay, that only love can build. A bond strong enough to surpass the barrier between life and the spirit world was exactly the type of bond between these two.

Zerell also mentioned a dream he had not too long after Gehrig passed. He dreamed that he and Gehrig had both passed the police test and were in uniform and on duty sharing a patrol car. The shift was uneventful, and Gehrig gave Zerell a ride home when it ended. He let Zerell out of the car, and then Z looked back at him and saw he wasn't in uniform anymore. Instead he was wearing jeans and a white t-shirt along with an old green shamrock ball cap. He said clearly to Zerell, "Everything is going to be fine."

The weird part is that the hat Z dreamed about was a hat Gehrig had given him some eight years ago. Zerell remembers being frustrated because he hadn't seen this hat in nearly five years. Even after moving, he had no idea where it was or even where to look for it. Yet when he awoke, he was clutching the lost hat in his hands! He cannot explain how this happened, but Zerell won't let that hat escape his grasp ever again.

Della Timmons, Gehrig's Mother

Della has had two very real experiences, only one was a dream. She dreamed her brother and she were driving in her car. Now Della (and everyone else) couldn't tell the difference between Angus and Gehrig's voice on the phone; they sounded exactly the same. She feels that's why Angus was with her so that she'd know. Her phone rings and Gehrig is on the other end but was using his eight-year-old voice, as if to make sure she'd not confuse them. Gehrig told her, "I'm all better now mom!"

Gehrig had suffered terribly with epilepsy for the last seven years of his life, and we both think this was what he was referring to. I must add that in the final five months of his life he had been seizure free. We like to think that he'd overcome this severe handicap or at least was finally able to control it.

Della's next experience came while texting her sister, Louise, another one of Gehrig's many aunts. She simply texted her sister to say, "Mom and I are going to physical therapy. I will call you when we're through." Somehow during their short texting the message became, "I'm so sorry you have to work so hard, SSR is asking that of Gehrig."

Although these words kept being added to the messages, neither sister ever typed them. Neither sister, nor anyone else, has been able to figure out the meaning of the additional words. Both are sure they came from Gehrig. So often people can't remember the entire dream or even understand the dreams or visits, but not being able to understand all the messages doesn't make them less valuable.

Natalie Kilburn, Gehrig's Sister

I don't think my son ever called Natalie anything but Nat. Natalie has had two dreams about Gehrig. The first she dreamed she was waiting for him to walk through Nana's front door. She saw the handle turn slowly and in walked Anthony (another cousin) and behind him she saw Gehrig.

Natalie said, "He walked in and had that Gehrig smile. His eyes twinkled and his face crinkled in his own special way. I miss seeing those things and hearing his voice so much. In my dream his smile was so huge and vibrant, and he made me feel like everything was okay. It was like when he talked I heard him, but not with my ears. I heard him inside my mind."

In the next dream Nat is once again waiting for him to come home but is in a mountain cabin this time. When he enters, he has that bigger-than-life-itself smile on his face—peaceful and knowing. He looks at me and says, "It's all fake, Nat, none of this is real!"

He tells her once more that it's all fake and none of this experience is real. Neither dream was like any other she'd ever had. It was so real and she believes it was a communication from her brother and that he's telling us it's all okay because he's okay. He's also saying that this existence is the dream and wherever he is, that's the reality.

The third thing that happened to Nat wasn't a dream. She had been hiking at Red Rocks, a place G truly loved, and as she was driving home she became overwhelmed with a feeling Gehrig was there. Here is what she said about the experience. "I looked up and saw a green cloud. This was an opal green, and the cloud looked like oil and water in the sky, and it was all very green. I've never seen a green cloud before or since, and I continued to look at it. I took my polarized sunglasses off, yet the color and tones stayed exactly the same. I just knew it was Gehrig and started talking to him; I thanked him and told him how much I miss him. He was so full of love, more so than anyone I know. It still hurts me terribly to not see that special twinkle in his eyes or the crinkles on his face, when his smile would light any room. The cloud pretty much followed me home."

Angus Timmons, Gehrig's Uncle and second Dad

Angus and Gehrig were very close, and I've said many times that Angus was Gehrig's second dad. He always called his uncle, Uncle Angy. In the first weeks after G had passed, Angus had a very intense and real dream. He dreamt he was in a beautiful park and saw a bench surrounded by people. As he approached, he saw there was a young man sitting on the bench putting his shoes on. It was obvious that the crowd around the young man knew and liked him. As Angus got closer he saw it was Gehrig on the bench, and Angus felt so relieved and happy. He hugged and kissed G who said, "Uncle Angy! Did you hear I faked my own death and I'm still alive?" (Can it really be coincidence that Gehrig used the word fake when describing his death with different people and in different dreams, as well as the park with a park bench setting?)

Angus felt such joy and happiness and told Gehrig, "We need to call your parents. They are going to be so relieved and happy to hear you are alive!" The dream ended at that point, but I knew as soon as he told me the story that he had indeed been visited by my son, and that my son was saying to him, and all of us, that death is more of a beginning than an end. The intense and unbearable pain of losing a child is something our loved ones don't want us to endure, so they come to us in our dreams, or in short glimpses of visions, desperately trying to ease our stifling burden.

Dustin Timmons, Gehrig's Cousin

Dustin and Gehrig considered themselves more brothers and friends than cousins. Dustin looked up to Gehrig, and Gehrig cared deeply for Dustin; he was always there for him. Dustin has had several messages and several visions from the big brother he never had and cousin he was closest to, Gehrig. Needless to say, my son's passing was extremely painful for so many of us, and it was terribly painful for Dustin. Once Gehrig passed, Dustin's life slowly began to change, for the better. And along every step of his journey, Dustin has seen Gehrig, far too many times to count.

Dustin has seen Gehrig standing on the side of the road waving and giving Dustin the thumbs up. Two of the most vivid visions were in a grocery store and another in the middle of his work day. Dustin was humping railroad ties while building a few hundred feet of track when he looked down the tracks. Just past where they ended stood his cousin, G, waving at him and giving him the thumbs up again while smiling ear to ear. Dustin's eyes immediately filled with tears and he fell to his knees.

His co-workers gathered around and said, "What's wrong?" Dustin replied, "You see that guy down there at the end of the tracks giving me the thumbs up? That is my cousin!"

His coworkers were perplexed and answered that there wasn't anyone down there, nor had they seen anyone else all day. Dustin realized it was yet another of his many visions.

Another humorous vision occurred in the grocery store. Dustin was trying to find a special BBQ sauce and was having trouble locating it when he looked down the aisle and saw G pointing at the correct stuff. Of course once he'd picked it up Gehrig was gone.

To me, it's yet another example of love being more powerful than death.

Mary Timmons, Gehrig's Aunt

Mary prays to begin each day and uses her small collection of prayer cards, which include Gehrig's memorial prayer card. She dreamed she was getting ready to pray and Gehrig was sitting on the edge of her bed holding all the prayer cards. He slowly passed five cards to her, but when she looked at the cards to see which ones he'd handed her, he was gone.

Lynn Kilburn, Gehrig's Paternal Grandmother, and Maternal Grandmother Nana Timmons (Anne)

Both of Gehrig's grandmothers had similar dreams or visitations. Both came very early in the morning just before they awoke. Nana saw Gehrig in her doorway arching his back against the jam wearing a gigantic smile. Nana said, "Oh Gehrig, is your back bothering you again?"

Gehrig didn't answer. He just continued smiling large at her and started doing his pushups. Then he disappeared as fast as he'd appeared.

Lynn Kilburn's visitation, likewise, happened just before she awoke one morning when she saw him standing by a terrace and once again smiling at her. He gave a long wave and said, "Hi grandma!" and that was it.

Within just a few days of G's passing, Lynn found herself walking downtown where a major construction project was happening. As Lynn began crossing the street, she became confused and found herself in traffic in front of a median. She felt a moment of panic, not knowing what she should do or which way she needed to go to avoid being hit.

At that exact moment she looked up and saw her grandson waving at her and pointing which way she should go. As the traffic whizzed by dangerously close, she made it to the median safely. When she looked up again Gehrig was gone. He seems to show up when people are in some form of distress or when he's most needed.

Nana, along with her dream, had another amazing and unbelievable experience. Nana had told her old friend Mary about Gehrig's death and sent her his prayer card. Mary stuck it to her fridge. Years before, Mary had told Nana about a Saint named Saint Maria Goretti from Portugal. Maria had been raped and murdered, yet came to her murderer in a dream and forgave him. Upon hearing the story, my son became extremely interested in Saint Maria Goretti and read all he could about her.

Mary's daughter was likewise fascinated by this particular saint and, as a young girl with severe and permanent back pain, experienced a miraculous healing while praying with her mother in front of a Saint Goretti relic. It was Mary's daughter who was visited by my son. While Mary was out of town her daughter stopped by uninvited to surprise her mom and spend the night. With her mom gone she just went to bed.

When Mary's phone rang at midnight she said it scared her, and when she saw it was her daughter she was even more hesitant to answer, but she did. Her daughter told her that she'd come for a visit and was staying at Mary's house. When she was there, she had a dream about a young man she thought may have been the grandson of Mary's old friend from Colorado; the one who'd just passed, and that it was such a real dream she had to call her mom.

She explained that she was in a beautiful park when a young man walked up to her and sat down next to her on the bench (yet another park scene with a bench). He turned toward her and said, "I want to thank you for inspiring me to take an interest in Saint Maria Goretti!"

She told her mother how real this dream was and how well she could remember it. Her mom told her to go to the kitchen and look on the refrigerator door; after moving something out of the way she found Gehrig's prayer card and excitedly stated, "Oh my God, it's him!"

She explained to her mom that the picture was the same young man who had just come to her in her dream. Mary called Nana the next day and there were many tears shed.

Like every day, we all still cry for the young man in Mary's daughter's dream and always will. There can only be one explanation for dreaming of someone you have never met or seen and then finding out through a photo that not only was the person real but that he was passed on as well. I believe it can only mean that people live on in the next realm. What other possible explanation could there be?

Why did both grandmothers have similar dreams? I have no answers for you, but the theme or pattern I'm picking up on is one of "Hey guys, chins up. I am okay and doing well, so don't be sad anymore!"

Like so many others in Gehrig's family, these experiences have all felt way too real to be called dreams. Both Lynn and Nana said it happened just before they opened their eyes and were no longer sleeping, adding to the many similarities other friends and families have experienced.

Abigail, Gehrig's Cousin

Another one of Gehrig's cousins is named Abigail. She and her husband were traveling through Alaska shortly after G's death when a frustrating trip turned worse and made them distraught. They were all out of cash when the trailer broke down. While her husband tried to negotiate a deal to fix the trailer, Abby walked into the bar. Her spirit was lifted as soon as she walked into the tavern, for this was a fishermen's bar and it was full of fishermen. Abby saw that the walls were fully ordained and covered with memorials, prayer cards, even money in some cases. She knew immediately she had to put her cousin's prayer card on the wall, so she quickly returned to the car.

Just before opening the car door she spied a crisp $20 bill lying right by the car door. Only her and her husband's footprints were visible around the car. She grabbed the money and card and went back in the bar. As she pulled G's prayer card out, it came out backwards. She realized immediately that he was telling her to put it up backwards so that whoever looks at it will read the fisherman's prayer. (His photo is on the front and the fisherman's poem is printed on the back of his prayer card.) Abby put the card up the way her cousin wanted and from that point on their trip was without incident.

These are only SOME of the unexplainable experiences G's friends and family have had. Some people were not comfortable sharing, while others preferred to keep their experiences private. Some have had too many to include each one, and I was unable to speak with several other friends of G. I would estimate that you are reading less than half of the experiences people have had.

Hearing from so many people who were so close to my son has helped me in many ways. It confirms that my son is still around. Only his body died, and he does not want his loved ones to suffer more than is necessary. That he was loved by so many more people than I or even he was aware of is so reassuring, and that he's still with us lessens my worry. What else can "I faked my death" possibly mean but that death is not something we need to fear?

There are somewhere between 54 and 57 mountains over 14,000 feet in Colorado, and I've spread my son's ashes on six of them. If I ever manage to climb and spread his ashes on all of the 14,000 footers, then there are some 200 peaks over 13,000 feet; and that will surely keep me occupied for the rest of my life. I do this with and for my son so that whenever I think about him or talk about him, I will be looking upwards, toward a snow-covered summit, so all his friends and family will always look upwards also towards his everlasting spirit.

Chapter Twelve

GINGER

<u>Quinton's Lesson</u>: Pets continue to exist as well!

Up to this point I have focused on visits from deceased humans. This can be a big enough hurdle for many people. When some try to share visits from their deceased loved ones they are told, "Don't tell anyone that; they will think you are crazy!" But what about pets? Well, how far down the rabbit hole do you want to go? I have to admit, when I used to hear of pet mediums, I was somewhat dismissive and never gave it much thought. I am ashamed to say that after all that I have seen and learned on this journey. I can still be skeptical, just because I haven't experienced it or heard of it before. Relating to pets on the other side, my skepticism was replaced with even more awe, courtesy of our cat, Ginger, who had something special in store for the entire family.

Ginger was a female orange tabby who was a fixture in our family for more than 10 years. She routinely roamed the forest, played with the kids and tormented the dogs. As Ginger aged, she would cuddle with us more and more. We noticed the difference; as I write this I realize her cuddling coincided with Quinton's departure, meaning she cuddled more with us during the last two years of her life.

We are pet lovers and have had some bad experiences with other cats, so we developed certain steps to minimize the potential for accidents. We learned to keep our master closet doors closed in our Conifer home because Ginger loved being in the closet and would hide behind the clothes on the lower rack. Invariably we would close the doors behind us only to return hours later and discover she was trapped in the closet. She never did have an accident in the closet, but we understood the potential for that happening, so we tried to keep the doors closed at all times.

Quinton and Ginger

Quinton's Legacy

We brought home two Puggles in November of 2006–a female and a male named Honey and Oatey. They were puppies, and Ginger immediately let them know she was the boss. Ginger was especially tough on Honey, who had been scratched enough on the nose to always tread carefully around Ginger. The dogs have always insisted on being where we are, so whenever we walk down the hall to the bedroom or another part of the house, they follow. Invariably Ginger would park herself in the middle of the hall, sitting on her haunches and I think even smiling a bit, if a cat can actually smile. We would walk past her and not long after Oatey would follow, but not Honey. Honey would pace back and forth in front of Ginger, moaning and crying to get past. It really was comical and often we would have to escort Honey past Ginger. This was the norm for the entire time we had all three of them.

Ginger also had some other interesting habits; one was using the corner of a wall leading into our kitchen as a rubbing post. She rubbed herself against it, firmly and vigorously several times a day. For most of the time we were in our Conifer mountain home, we had this wall painted a dark, forest green, but after we expanded in 2007 to make room for our nephew, I had repainted the wall white. In a very short period of time her rubbing turned the corner a dark brownish grey color. I would clean it and repaint it on occasion, but it didn't matter; it would be dark again soon.

On August 24, 2011, Ginger went out to play in the yard as she had always done but didn't come in that night. Quinton had already transitioned and demonstrated repeatedly that he still exists. Kristine and I called for Ginger to no avail. I do remember hearing one "meow" that night, but only one, and it was different. It was as if it was in my mind and not my ear. The date coincided with Kristine's trip to visit with her mom in Phoenix. The next day I took her to the airport; still no Ginger. We still had a couple of days until the weekend and I had to work, so I didn't have any time to really search for what I suspected would be her body. To be truthful, we didn't expect to find her since coyotes and mountain lions are prevalent in our area.

The weekend arrived. I was chopping and stacking wood for the upcoming winter. While I worked I noticed what looked like a rag or shirt of some sort in the yard. Walking over to investigate, I realized that I had found Ginger. Something had caught her and disemboweled her. It just broke my heart; she was such a good cat and such a part of our family. Part of me thought, *first Quinton and now Ginger, this is so disheartening.* Cheyanne was home so I asked her to stand with me and say some words after I buried her deep in the yard. Cheyanne was pretty choked up, so I joked that I am sure Ginger would still be around tormenting the dogs. I was joking; I really didn't expect that would occur. I was in for a big surprise!

After Ginger had transitioned, the dogs were the first to see Ginger. This wasn't much of a surprise given we had learned that animals have an easier time seeing spirits. Honey and Oatey had demonstrated this as they both noticed Quinton in the house one evening as we were downstairs watching movies just a few short weeks after Quinton transitioned. All of us, (Kristine, Cheyanne, TK and I) sat looking at the TV while the dogs, especially Oatey for some reason, stared intently in a corner of the family room. They kept staring and fidgeting. They saw something, but maybe their dog minds just could not understand what it was, or maybe they knew it was Quinton in spirit! We have since heard of this phenomenon over and over; pets see spirit while humans could not. It is truly amazing how often it happens and how many books have been written about that happening, or at least discussed within books relating to the transition of someone.

Not long after Ginger passed, Honey started acting really weird. What was weird was that while we recognized her behavior, the stimulus for her behavior was seemingly no longer present. Honey would attempt to follow us down the hall, but stop in the middle of the hall, whining and crying while refusing to go any further. We knew Ginger was there in spirit, still tormenting the heck out of Honey. This continued for the next 16 months, only seemingly coming to an end when we sold the home and moved out in December of 2012. It really does boggle the mind when you sit and think about it. To Honey, Ginger was there! While I am no expert, I can reasonably expect that to Ginger, she was there too. Before all of this happened, we would have thought death meant that none of this was possible; now we know otherwise.

What really surprised me was the fact that Kristine and I saw Ginger, too. For some reason, I just didn't think being able to see, hear and sense Quinton in spirit would apply to a pet transitioning. I don't recall seeing any of the previous pets in my lifetime that had died in spirit form, so I really wasn't expecting to see Ginger. Like I said, there are no rules to seeing our deceased loved ones, no rhyme and no reason; now I realize that it isn't any different for pets.

One early morning I walked past our master closet on the way to the bathroom and noticed one of the closet doors was ajar, which I found odd since we still had a routine of keeping them closed. When I walked back the other way, I opened the door further and saw what appeared to be one of my white socks stretched out on the floor. The room was very dark, almost black, but I saw the white sock; it was kind of luminous. Turning the light on I looked where the sock had been and nothing was there. I quickly surmised it was Ginger. She got in the closet again after all!

I told Kristine of what I saw and she shared that she had seen Ginger rubbing on the corner of the wall in the kitchen just like she always did. Where I saw Ginger glowing in the dark, Kristine saw Ginger in the day light while awake and could actually see here moving as she rubbed herself on the corner. Kristine further shared that she could hear Ginger's meow in the house too!

For those of you who like watching scary movies or program that aired from 2005 until 2010, Ghost Whisperer, you might be inclined to think Ginger, or Quinton for that matter, would stay with the house after we left. But it doesn't work like that – in our case anyway. Now that we are in our Peoria, Arizona home, both of us have seen Quinton and Ginger out of the corners of our eyes.

As time has passed since we discovered that pets sometimes visit, we have since learned that many already know this, and books have been written. Kind of funny, once you are opened up to accept new truths, more evidence of these truths suddenly is noticed for the first time, even though it was there all along. This reminds me of the Buddhist proverb, "When the student is ready, the teacher will appear." To that point, whenever Kristine and I attend a conference about death and communications with those on the other side, there is always a breakout session relating to pets. Renowned author Anne Puryear, who wrote a book titled *Stephen Lives: His Life, Suicide and Afterlife*, recently started a group on Facebook called Helping Pet Lovers Heal, which is patterned after a support group that we are a part of, Helping Parents Heal (www. helpingparentsheal.info). The common bond between the groups is both encourage the sharing of our deceased loved ones making contact.

Chapter Thirteen

OUR GRANDSON

Quinton's Lesson: Don't beat yourself up Dad, you have another chance!

Cheyanne had a tough go after her brother Quinton transitioned. Honestly, at times I didn't think she would ever recover. She was lost and afraid, often. She watched Kristine and me growing, evolving and ultimately touching others, lifting others while she wondered what was wrong with her. I shared before that Cheyanne has the gift – she is intuitive – but she is afraid of it and therefore hasn't been willing to refine it or even manage it yet. After Quinton passed, and to an extent still, she cannot sit in silence. For her, there is too much going on in the silence.

She finished her high school education back in Conifer. When she studied she would have the TV on and her headphones in playing music to avoid the silence and what she might find there. She became quite self-destructive with various substances used to calm her nerves and help her lose weight. She had on again and off again relationships, but she was just passing the time with them trying to further numb her pain. Kristine would fight her every step of the way, knowing that the potentially destructive decisions Cheyanne was making had consequences, while I focused on simply loving her and hoping she would see her way out of it.

She ended up in one relationship with a man and she blossomed. We could not believe the transformation. Suddenly she was trying to be part of a committed relationship, at least from outward appearance. But this fellow was scarred and carried several suitcases of baggage. Thankfully that relationship ended. Cheyanne came to me, as she sometimes does when she needs to hear hard truths, and asked what I thought. She had already told me how he made her feel, how he belittled her, put her down and made her fearful. I just reminded her that she already knew what she had to do, and to do so face to face. She did and it was over, thankfully, and then a wonderful thing happened.

While Kristine and I wondered what might happen after that "test relationship" ended, she didn't stumble too far. In fact, during this time frame she experienced quite an epiphany herself that thankfully didn't result in the death of another or too much damage to her vehicle. She, like so many, is accustomed to driving while multi-tasking. On this particular day, she blacked out and essentially woke up as she was trying to steer the car back onto the road as it nearly ended up in a creek. It was quite the wakeup call and reminded her of Quinton and Amanda. Not long after, she met someone very special and fell in love. Today, Salvador Garcia-Franco is our son-in-law and father to our grandson.

Cheyanne met Salvador while working at Three Garcia's in Conifer where he was the cook and she waited tables. They hit it off and six months later they were married. Salvador is the hardest working young man I know, coupled with being wise and patient; I actually find myself admiring him. He is six and a half years older than Cheyanne, and is exactly what she needs – a loving, patient, gentleman to help her dispense of her own luggage. They married on November 1, 2012 and rented a single bedroom apartment, then quickly discovered they were pregnant. We were going to be grandparents!

The nine-and-a-half months passed quickly. We had moved back to Arizona but visited often. Salvador, being quite wise, purchased a

Pekinese female puppy named Cholula, who melted her heart and kept Cheyanne company while he worked.

The baby, we soon discovered, was going to be a little boy, and he was due to be born in July 2013! Kristine, Nellie and Cheyanne started throwing names around and by May, while searching a database, Nellie found the name Savion. Everyone took a liking to the name and, subsequently, we discovered that Savion means "new house." This felt right to us because our grandson represented not only a new house (new beginning) to us, but to Cheyanne as well. Yes, Quinton's name was in the mix, but there just is no replacing our son. But our grandson's middle name was to be Quinton. For the better part of two months we called him Savion Quinton Garcia. But as the day of his birth approached, Salvador shared that his family had a tradition that the first born in each son's new family take his father's name. Savion Quinton became Salvador Quinton, but we know that he represents a new beginning, a new house to both bloodlines.

July rolled around and all of us were beyond excited. For Cheyanne, it was more than just excitement; the weather had warmed and she was hot, wanting for her son to be born as soon as possible! We had been searching for starter homes to buy for them in hopes that we could find the right house and take possession before our grandson was born. But with the rapidly improving residential real estate market, inventory was very low resulting in bidding wars on every house that we looked at. Kristine and I wanted to be close and get out of the heat in Phoenix, so we rented a condo in Evergreen for the entire month of July. Arriving in Evergreen on July 2nd, we settled in. We spent time with Cheyanne and Salvador during the first couple weeks, which was wonderful, but no baby. He had to cook a while longer, and he had a surprise for all of us.

On July 17, we got the call – well, actually it was "calls." Both Cheyanne and Salvador tried to call us on our cell phones starting at 4:00 a.m., but we didn't hear our phones until 7:00 am. It was time, and they were going to the hospital. Cheyanne, who had been in labor since midnight, was in contact with the nurses who monitored her progress and finally told them to come in at 7:00 a.m. Cheyanne and Salvador were admitted to a pre-delivery room around 8:00 a.m., while we arrived shortly after 9:00 a.m. The timing of our arrival was perfect. Just a few short minutes after we arrived, a delivery room was made available, and all of us went up to the second floor and settled in.

Cheyanne's pain level was increasing dramatically by 10:30 a.m. The nurses asked if Cheyanne wanted an epidural and immediately she answered, "Yes!" By noon, the epidural had been administered and everybody relaxed. Cheyanne was ready to take a nap, and for that matter, so was Salvador. We turned out the lights and left them to give them their space. At 3:30 p.m. we came back, peeking in on them we saw the lights were still off and both were sleeping soundly. Next, we went to the waiting room that was pretty full of grandparents and relatives waiting for new family additions. I promptly made myself comfortable and fell asleep, snoring loudly Kristine tells me. At 4:30 p.m., we went back to check on them again and were greeted by an entirely different scene.

Everyone in our little family was born in the nine o'clock hour except me – I was born at 4:10 p.m. Cheyanne was born at 9:42 a.m., Quinton was born at 9:37 p.m., and Kristine was born at 9:40 a.m. I expected that our grandson would be born during the nine o'clock hour as well. As we walked back into Cheyanne's delivery room, the room was abuzz. The lights were on; there was a nurse in there checking Cheyanne and pronounced she had reached full dilation. At that point, I thought Salvador Quinton would make his entrance during the six o'clock hour. I was wrong. Between 4:30 p.m. and 5:00 p.m., the activity level in the room tripled with three nurses present, gowned up and ready to go. At 5:05 p.m. I looked up at the clock and started crying as I realized that our grandson was going to be born during the same hour in the afternoon that our son departed. What are the odds?

Quinton's Legacy

We were all up and finding positions to assist without hampering the nurses. Cheyanne's husband was on her left side to hold her left leg while Kristine was on Cheyanne's right side to hold her right leg. I had positioned myself in the only spot I could find, by Cheyanne's right ear. At 5:35 p.m. I looked up while Cheyanne gathered herself for another push. Just then, I saw the picture of Quinton that Cheyanne had brought with them on the mantle directly behind her, and I started to cry again. I looked right, into my son-in-law's eyes, and continued crying. Quinton was there with us! This realization hit me with its full force as the nurses were telling Cheyanne how close she was and guided her right hand down between her legs to feel the crown of her son's head.

This is my part in the tale. At this point I spoke directly into Cheyanne's right ear, telling her that all she needed was to give us one more really huge push and she would be done. I might have even told her to give us a Godzilla push. Moments before she had been saying she was too tired to push anymore, which naturally reminded me of a Bill Cosby skit from the 80s; no I didn't tell her this in the moment. I told her one more giant push and she delivered on that push and delivered her son!

Just like that—he was born. Within seconds he seemingly soundlessly began breathing without a slap or a wail; within 15 minutes he was having his first meal. He is amazing. His dad calls him Salvador while his uncles call him Quinton. We have accidently called him Savion a few times, but usually call him Salvador Q. One thing is for certain, he is a very calm and happy baby boy! He is something of a Buddha boy, as he is so calm and peaceful, and when we hold him we become even more calm and peaceful. He is always is smiling!

Cheyanne and Salvador Quinton

Yes, we are proud grandparents! While many tease us that we are too young to be grandparents, we have enough aches, pains and gray hair to fit the bill. This young man completes us, in a way, the closing of a chapter and beginning anew. We enjoy every moment we have with him! He is having the same effect on Cheyanne and Salvador Sr.! They have every reason to be happy and proud to have him as a son. And the beat goes on . . . .

A year passed, and our grandson Salvador Quinton is growing up. He turned one year old on July 17, 2014, and he is even more amazing each time we are blessed to be in his presence. We saw him in April for Easter, May for Cheyanne's birthday, and then on our annual trip to Rocky Point, Mexico during the first week in June. And words just don't do justice when trying to explain him as only a grandparent can, but I will tell you what is in my heart.

Sal Q is present. He is 100 percent in the here and now, seemingly seeing everything. I know all kids are present like that, a fact that I didn't appreciate when I helped raise Quinton and Cheyanne, but I do now—as I suspect most grandparents do. Being in his presence lifts my soul; being in his presence is an opportunity to help him keep his gifts from heaven intact, and being in his presence is where we belong. The same is true for all grandparents.

I picked up Cheyanne and Sal Q from the airport in early June 2014. I pulled up along the curb where I expected them to come out, climbed out of our Hyundai Sonata and began trying to install the car seat. The key word is trying. As I did so, they came up upon me. After hugging Cheyanne, I looked at my grandson who was in a bit of a daze, given his day had started so early. At first he looked at me like I was something of a stranger. I moved closer, my smile even larger and he lit up like a Christmas tree – his smile matching mine; he even started clapping his hands to show his pleasure of seeing me. Yes, I expect you may be able to accurately imagine how that makes me feel.

The next day we headed south to Rocky Point where we stayed for five days. Five days with our grandson, being with him, interacting with him and watching him. He is so joyous! He dances! And I dance with him (nobody has gotten me to dance, but I dance with my grandson). He is joyous when he dances, moving to the music, not caring a bit if the steps are right. Well, I certainly don't want him to have my curse of worrying about such mundane things as steps and rhythm, so I dance with him in my arms, and sometimes he bounces on the floor, feeling the music and being joyous. He is a gift to us.

His smile is infectious. It is so genuine, free and easy. He sees who is in front of him and he smiles, smiles big! But there is something else he does that just lights my fire and boggles my mind. At that time, he wasn't walking consistently, but he crawled everywhere. He can sit up on his knees, rocking, bouncing and dancing, but when he gets really excited he will do all of that on this knees at the same time he wildly swings his arms from side to side. Words don't do it justice. His arms look like that of a rag doll as he is laughing and giggling, all at the same time. Can you imagine being so joyous? As he carries on so, we are laughing and giggling too, right along with him; the gift of life embodied. He is a reminder to us all of just how joyous life can be.

At one point, Cheyanne was in the resort pool with Sal Q in his float. Cheyanne had her back to us, so I decided to have a little fun. The waterfall was on as I slipped into the pool and slowly, ever so slowly made my way over to them. As Cheyanne turned slightly I adjusted my position with the hope that she wouldn't notice me, while trying to catch Sal Q's eye. This went on for some time, until finally he saw me standing right behind Cheyanne and again lit up like a Christmas tree. Naturally, at that point Cheyanne, realizing someone was behind her, turned around. It is that reaction of seeing each of us that is truly the most amazing feeling. He looks at everyone that way – in the morning, after a nap – any time, every time.

He has the gift, the gift of being loved unconditionally and completely. So calm, sweet and present; rarely does he cry and rarely does he get frazzled. He must be an old soul and yes, he does remind us of our son, Quinton, his Uncle Q.

Quinton's Legacy

Quinton is a gift to all of us and so is Sal Q! Holding him soothes my soul. When he is wound up and raring to go, it's as if he's saying, "Turn the music on. Let's get this party started! A little louder, please!"

Chapter Fourteen

QUINTON'S GIFT

Quinton's Lesson: Continue to pay attention!

You just never know what is going to happen on any given day. Some days can bring you struggles and others will bring something truly amazing. All too often we focus on the challenges and dismiss the good, or worse, don't even see it. We are tasked with paying attention with our hearts and minds, listening for that still small voice that tugs at our consciousness. The more often we can do this, the better the chance of experiencing something truly wonderful, as we experienced on April 14 of 2014.

Kristine and I continue down a more spiritual path, taking opportunity to attend events that feed our souls. Dr. Eben Alexander, author of *Proof of Heaven,* came to our church, The Unity Church of Phoenix, on April 14. Dr. Alexander's book is quite profound. At times in his life he was an agnostic, meaning he was skeptical of what we have come to know as truth. This makes his journey all the more remarkable.

We were excited to attend, even after a long day. We had planned on seeing Elizabeth Boisson, our friend and co-founder of the parent support group Helping Parents Heal, aka Parents United in loss (www.helpingparentsheal.info). We knew she would be there and were looking forward to catching up with her. Elizabeth came with a woman we didn't know, Susanne Wilson. As we stood in a short line waiting for the doors to open, Elizabeth not only mentioned that Suzanne was a

145

medium, she also shared that she had brought her deceased son Morgan through to her in an incredible way with many validating statements. In short, Elizabeth indicated that Susanne had remarkable gifts. (To learn more about Susanne, go to www.carefreemedium.com)

When I meet mediums who are off the clock, so to speak, I make it point to not expect, or ask anything about Quinton. Being mediums, I expect they get that all the time and I further expect it sometimes becomes a burden. We didn't want to make her uncomfortable or have her thinking, "Here we go again." We didn't want to come across as needy, not that we are, but when you have lost a child you always want more! More visits, more signs and more dreams! Both Kristine and I acknowledged what we heard, were happy to meet her and collectively we went on to other topics.

The doors opened and we filed in. The sanctuary is divided into four sections running north-south with those four split in the middle making eight sections. The four of us went toward the same section nearest the front. We weren't trying to sit next to Elizabeth and Suzanne, but that was exactly what happened. They entered the row from the west, and we entered the same row from the east, and we ended up sitting together with Susanne and Kristine adjacent to one another. Dr. Alexander came out on the stage and began his presentation.

Kristine and I resonated with everything he had to say, and his effect on those in attendance was remarkable. During the break, you could hear the conversations about the beyond and the hereafter. I was taking it all in, but there was a group sitting behind me that I listened closely to, nodding my head and silently agreeing. After a while, I had to join in and share a bit of our journey with them. The break ended and next came a demonstration put on by Karen Newell.

During the last session with Karen, I noticed Susanne had become distracted and was scribbling notes on a piece of paper. I paid no attention, and it never even crossed my mind that someone may have made contact with her. I knew nothing about Susanne or how she worked. The last session ended and the folks behind me wanted to know more about Quinton's visits, so I did my best to fill them in. I say did my best because something pretty amazing was happening just beside me, and Kristine summed it up wonderfully on Facebook that night. It was subsequently shared on the Helping Parents Heal Facebook page, which is shared below:

What an amazing presentation Dr. Eben Alexander, author of *Proof of Heaven* and Karen Newell put on last night. It was awesome being around so many people who have the same mindset. I have never once doubted that "There Is More," nor have I ever questioned where my loved ones have gone. The evening was simply amazing, but that was not the highlight. Our highlight of the evening is when Susanne Wilson, who is a medium, turned to us at the end of the evening and asked, "Can I share something with both of you?" Of course we were all ears.

She said, "Forty-five minutes into the presentation, Quinton came to me. He snapped his fingers and said, "Now I have your attention." Quinton would be getting his drivers permit this upcoming school year; he said he already knows how to drive. I validated it saying, yes, Quinton would be turning 15 this year. She went on to say that after the accident he was with Ernie Jackson. No doubt. I confirmed as Ernie Jackson wrote in his first book, *Quinton's Messages*, that he knew someone was holding his hand, but my husband had no idea this was possible. You see it wasn't until weeks after that he realized it was "Q" and that his reality of what he thought to be true would forever be changed. Susanne said he is the godfather and wants to know if you know what that means, while my friend Elizabeth Veney Boisson and I discussed that, indeed, I knew what that meant. He is the godfather to his sister Cheyanne Cano-Garcia's beautiful baby boy Salvador Quinton. She mentioned he is going to be a doctor. This didn't surprise me because he is an intelligent young man, loved helping and making people better.

Lastly, she said, "He's showing me a yellow dump truck." I confirmed that when we bought the house for Cheyanne and her family in Aurora, Colorado, there was a small yellow dump truck left in the back yard. The couple we bought from had no kids. Quinton did get to experience riding and driving in a huge yellow crane truck at our neighbor's house (Rob and Mindy Johns – Rob owns his own excavation company and did the excavation for their new home. Quinton and I would go over there every day to check the progress) when they were working on their new house. She went on to say he is a gentle soul and has been with us the entire evening. He must have been that beautiful bird we saw flying over us while we enjoyed our Sushi at Unity Church before the event. This was the highlight. Susanne knew nothing about us except that we lost our son. She asked nothing of us, except for our time to relay her message. This is the power of our loved ones and the souls that have been given the gift to communicate with the "other side." Q has tremendously blessed us and we know that there is no goodbye like I mentioned to my friend, Vickie Baroch. It is until we meet again. I just had to share, so thank you for taking the time to read. Many blessings to you, and may your life be full of love and light."

The day after the meeting I told Cheyanne about our evening the night before. As I spoke to her I remembered something, or maybe it was Quinton reminding me that when we purchased the home in Colorado for them, there was a yellow Tonka toy earth mover in the back yard and on the deck. It just came to me that this was left for his godson Salvador Quinton, that it was a gift to him. As I realized this and said it out loud to Cheyanne, I started crying.

All of this is amazing and wonderful in and of itself, but we had two more validations coming. As part of the subsequent sharing and posting, a picture was posted of the yellow toy we discovered and that Cheyanne now keeps in Salvador Quinton's bedroom. That picture is below and at some point Susanne Wilson saw it and commented, "That is what I saw."

Yellow Tonka toy

There was one additional validation! When Quinton came through to Susanne, she shared that he was snapping this fingers. This is so Quinton! He always struggled to snap his fingers and would actually practice as he became older, finally mastered the ability to do so. Once he had it figured out, he would snap his fingers often; for him to come to Suzanne in that way is profound and lets us know that it was really him!

Section Three

Our View of Life

Chapter Fifteen

GRIEVING AND THE HARD WORK OF SAVING A MARRIAGE

Quinton's Lesson: Marriage can survive adversity!

I am blessed to have Kristine as my wife, of that there is no doubt. She, on so many levels is the older soul than I and, subsequently, is here to show me something. She demonstrates love and strength in a relationship to me – always. This is why she is in my life; she has helped me and continues to show me the way.

A marriage takes two people who are committed to doing the hard work as each person grows and changes, even as they grow and change at different paces. Kristine does that hard work and is teaching me how to do it as well, consistently, day after day, year after year. Kristine is the emotional glue of our marriage, showing me how to feel my emotions more as she demonstrates the meaning of true commitment.

Any marriage takes hard work, but even more so after the death of a child. And if the two of you, suffering the death of a child, want to play the blame game, it is even harder. On some level, it boils down to a choice. Do you want to save your marriage after your world has been turned inside out, or is it easier to run from it? In the midst of our pain, we held it together. We could have lashed out at one another in an effort to purge some of that pain, but we chose not to – even in the heat of the moment. Often, it is more productive and wiser to be silent and let the moment pass instead of lashing out. Do you choose to stay to do the hard work, have the unbelievable tough conversations, or run from the pain?

It is because of my wife that I didn't run. She is the strength in our marriage, and in being the strength, she has taught me to do the same. Now *we* are the strength in our marriage. Below are her thoughts on what it took to hold us together.

I was asked to write this chapter because I have such a strong belief in working through every marriage challenge, and this, by far, has been the greatest. You have heard about me, as I have been quoted many times in *Quinton's Messages*, but you've never heard directly from me. I am the silent partner, so to speak, but on this subject – not so silent. You see, the topic of this book and the prior book have been primarily on my husband's journey of finding himself to heal from the loss of our son.

Let me start by saying that too many people go into marriage thinking it's going be easy. Guess what? It's not! There are ups and downs, and if you've read our first book, you know my husband had lots of baggage. Like they say, find someone who will accept you with all your baggage and help you unpack. Little did I know what I was in for at the young age of 19.

I was raised in a nurturing household with two parents who loved each other and most importantly instilled morals, values and, above all, love in me. When I got married, my parents had been married more than 25 years. Yes, they faced their challenges in marriage, but worked through them, and I am forever grateful for the lessons they taught. As children, we were never really included in the financial struggles or marriage difficulties; my parents kept that to themselves.

We all know that money is a big marriage destroyer, and not being on the same page as your spouse when it comes to the financials can ruin a marriage. We did face those challenges in our marriage, given that Ernie has always been the bread winner and very tight when it comes to spending. I have worked and contributed, but he definitely brought home the bacon. Let me tell you, those were some of the most difficult times in our marriage. I dreaded the budget conversations and feared the outcome each time. Yet money has not been our biggest challenge.

Nothing could have prepared me for dealing with the loss of my child and what it would do to my marriage. Everyone certainly had their two cents to put in and made sure to express, "You know most marriages don't last when a child has passed." I think, on some level, some wanted to see firsthand how we'd deal with the challenge.

As to be expected, Ernie and I grieved very differently. During this time, we withdrew from each other for the first six months. We had to adjust to a new normal. I cried (and cried) in my bedroom alone, all the while dealing as best I could with all of my own injuries from being run over and surviving this horrific accident. I was a mess. Ernie went into work mode from the day of the accident, and I don't believe, until now, that he has really given himself that time to grieve.

I was a mess. I was emotionally and physically destroyed. I was grateful that my injuries were tolerable, and with several doctors' appointments and months of therapy, I knew I would be okay. While Ernie was there for me during this time to take me to my appointments with the brain specialist, pain management specialist, regular physician, as well as follow-ups, he was not there for me emotionally. I became numb to the fact that my son was gone and spent several months medicated to deal with my pain.

While Ernie did not want to be left alone and kept busy, all I wanted was to be left alone to cry and try to process what the hell kind of nightmare I was living. I asked many times why I couldn't have been the one to go, and of course, I was told by many that it was not my time. The pain of it all was overwhelming at times, and that's when my mind questioned, *why had I survived this?* Well, now I know. I survived this because I had to be here for my daughter, who was just a wreck, and for my husband who needed me because he was a mess as well.

After being away from my family for 14 years, I wanted to be home with my mom in Arizona. I had already suffered the loss of my dad in 2003. I was away while my mom fought breast cancer in 2006, and then Quinton transitioned in 2009. I needed to be with family to heal. I am so blessed that after the accident, my mom stayed with us for a short time to help take care of me. Like I said, Ernie was there, but not really there. (Note from Ernie: Kristine and her Mom have the most amazing connection).

A few months after the accident, we decided that we would look for property in Arizona with the intention of living there again someday. You see, we were going to be receiving a large settlement on behalf of our son, and the only way I was comfortable taking this money that was given because our son had passed was to invest it in property where he longed to live – in Arizona with family. Shortly after we made this decision, Cheyanne, who was in her junior year of high school, decided she wanted to leave Colorado and live with my mom in Arizona. She could not handle living in the house she grew up in without her brother. She felt that escaping would make the pain go away.

We were fortunate to be looking for a home at this time when the market had fallen to an all-time low, and houses had rapidly depreciated. Luckily, we found a beautiful home, and after discussions with my mom, she agreed to move into it and Cheyanne would come live with her. Mom lived in a senior community prior to this, so there was no option for Cheyanne to live with her there. So it all worked out perfectly. I wanted to do whatever I could to help Cheyanne get through this difficult time.

Quinton's Legacy

We purchased our Arizona home in late December 2009 and after winter break, Cheyanne completed her second semester in January 2010. While this time together was good for all of us, the next months that Ernie and I had together were the most beneficial to our relationship. At this point, I had returned to work and Ernie had resigned from his job.

I went back to work primarily to keep my mind busy, but it wasn't working; I was in pain and distraught. Ernie, who was told by many to write a book about his life and what he survived, began to write *Quinton's Messages*. I decided that I could no longer keep working at the job I had loved for the last six years; I just couldn't handle everything the way I had prior to our accident. So in March I resigned and gave 90 days' notice.

At this point I knew what I needed to do for me and my family. I always put me last, but now I knew that I needed to get to Arizona so we could be a family again. By May, Ernie had gotten a new job and was back in the work force and my 90 days ended; I was walking away from a job I loved.

Ernie's work environment was a good place for him because he was among people he knew who could understand what he'd been through, and while working, he continued to write his book. The end of May came, and I was now a stay-at-home mom again–with no one to take care of but me and the dogs. This was very strange to me but very healing. We took our annual trip to Rocky Point as a family, but that year (2010) our purpose was mainly to celebrate and memorialize my dad and my son who passed six years and two days apart from one another. The trip was emotional, but all in all good for our family to reminisce these two loved ones.

Ernie's and my time came after returning from our vacation. We spent many nights together just holding each other. Of course, me sobbing buckets and Ernie (being the strong guy he is) holding it in. You see, we were trying to get used to this new normal that we were living. All of a sudden we are empty nesters; well not really, we still had our four-legged fur babies. I could not help but continue to think about the friends who said our marriage wouldn't withstand this loss. Well, we had celebrated yet another year of our, at that point, 18-year marriage. Our marriage has not been the easiest, but like they say, anything worthwhile is worth working for. And work I did! It seems I was always the one to work on our marriage, never willing to give in to those challenging times. I just felt I had given 18 years, why would I allow this to destroy us. That is not what my son would want.

Ernie will agree that I have always been the emotionally strong one when it comes to working through issues, as I have been dealing with his for many years. I have my own issues and he has been pretty patient with me too, but because of his childhood, mine can't compare to his. I had a strong sense that this was yet another challenge for me – to be *Strong Kristine*!

Strong, yes indeed, I needed to find my inner strength, because while I was a very strong, determined woman, I was very weak minded. It took me almost three years after the loss of Quinton to realize that he wants me to be strong, to find my inner strength. Time and time again, I asked this question, "Quinton, I know you planned this and left because it was the only way your dad would change, but what is there for me to learn?"

Well, let's just say I'm a little slow, but I did figure it out. After Q came to me in several visitations, it seemed he always said in some way, "BE STRONG MOM." Well, I am happy to say that I have found that inner and outer strength to be strong, to know my self-worth and to feel confident in my abilities.

While this horrific accident did take my son's body, it did not take his spirit! And while it left me somewhat medically disabled, I refuse to let that define me. I continue to honor my son and his departure, and I know that he wants me to be happy and not mourn his loss because, in time, we will be together.

Quinton's Legacy

Ernie and I celebrated our twenty-third anniversary this April 2015. I am happy to say that I truly believe the best is yet to come in our marriage. I honestly believe it gets better and better, and over the past five years it has! No marriage is perfect, and neither is ours. We will all go through struggles and face challenges, but in the end, my advice is to never lose hope. Have faith, and yes – be strong – and your strength will get you through.

Chapter Sixteen

CHEYANNE'S PAIN

Quinton's Lesson: Amidst pain, there is hope!

Our daughter's section is raw and painful, but it is real. The pain she shares below speaks a truth that I don't allude to, but it needs to be heard, as all of us feel it or should allow ourselves to feel it. The big picture is that ignoring the pain while focusing on the aha moments may make us easier to be around, but we do ourselves a disservice. In order to heal, these are emotions we have to come to terms with at some point, or we imprison ourselves mentally and emotionally. There is no magic wand and no set timetable for grieving. Here are her words:

> For those of you who have lost a sibling that made you an only child, you know the emptiness and loneliness I feel. You know how I feel out of place, like I don't belong anywhere I go. The years go by and it still hurts. I can try to numb the pain, confusion and emptiness I feel by focusing my attention elsewhere, but it's just always there. At the end of the inevitable high is a low that will leave you incapable of seeing the truth; a low so low that I am incapable of comprehending how I might get through it.
>
> During the years following my brother's death I focused my attention on the next high and how to keep them coming. I focused on starving myself and getting those butterflies back, thinking maybe if I achieved some societal image of perfection I would feel alive again. I focused on everything I

was able to control. I focused on anything that could make me feel something different than the hell I had been experiencing.

Highs and lows; I lived for the highs, recklessly throwing myself into the arms of men that never intended to love me. And if they did, it was only for a moment, until they realized how damaged I really was. The fear of being left completely alone took over my being. For years, I have surrounded myself with selfish people who only intend on taking care of themselves – just so I wouldn't have to be alone. I just kept telling myself to take one step at a time, but I whole heartedly gave myself completely to anything or anyone who promised a better moment or better tomorrow. Guy after guy, hit after hit, until I found myself back where I started, feeling lost and alone.

I am having such a hard time with this now because I cannot just turn to the same things I would in my past to numb the pain. I am a now a mother of one boy (and another on the way) and a wife. I am so desperately trying to grieve properly and be a mother my children will be proud of. I am constantly reminded of the doubt I have in myself and the people around me have; I don't honestly believe I can do this. It has been more than five years and in my darkest moments, it feels like I couldn't possibly forget the hurt and the nightmares of Quinton slipping away over and over again.

The person I trusted to numb me for the rest of my life has ripped open the wound and now patiently stands by me, helping me to stitch up the aching hole in my heart, only properly this time. I say that my husband ripped open my wound; I understand why most of you would consider this a terrible thing to say, so let me explain in what context my comment must be taken.

I believe that when married or in a committed relationship, this is the only way to know you are with the right person. I realized I was handling things all wrong in my past, numbing the pain when I should have been healing my wounds. My husband made me see that. Yes, it is painful to open the wound, but the wound is more of an abscess because it never really healed. I feel as if I need to grieve all over again, but this time let the emotions flow instead of running from them. I need to feel and acknowledge every emotion. I cannot cover it up and ignore it if I am to grow and learn. He, my husband, has opened my eyes and let me see I have every opportunity to do things in a different way. My husband is God sent; I may never completely understand what I did to deserve such a loving and patient man.

But the pain still remains. More than five years have passed since I last looked into my brother's eyes, and I sometimes feel even more lost and confused. I always thought by now I would be okay. I thought I wouldn't cry on a regular basis; I thought I wouldn't burst out in anger at one wrong glance. I believed I would have myself just a little bit together, but I didn't' know how I was going to get myself there. Today, I am nowhere-near close to being "there." I have taken everyone, well just about everyone out of my life that does not better me, leaving me with almost no one.

Most people see anger in me, but it is truly sadness and no one wants that in their life; hell, I don't want it in mine either. I wish I felt like my parents. It is really admirable and I pray that one day I can make it to a peaceful state of mind. I continue to experience my highs when my 19-month-old son gives me a hug, and every time he stops what he is doing to give me a kiss, and especially when he says, "La you!" I live for those moments. They numb my sadness if only for a moment.

Being alone in my car, listening to some good music with the bass turned up, distracts from all the noise and nonsense surrounding me. I especially like feeling my soon-to-be-born baby boy kick as he moves in my belly. He reminds me that there will be a better tomorrow because I have yet to see his face or cradle his small body. He reminds me with one little push that I am important too, and that someone needs me. That someone's life would be affected if I didn't wake up tomorrow. My sons remind me that I have a purpose, and there is so much more to come from this beautiful and painful life.

The years go by and it still hurts. Losing a sibling is something that will forever alter the way I feel and the way I see life. Sometimes the overwhelming emotions take my breath away; it is as if he was taken from us just yesterday.

We are so proud of our daughter Cheyanne for sharing her feelings. This sharing is the first step to finding peace, a deep soul level of peace that she wants, and we want for her. In reading her words, we as parents, Kristine and I, recognize the fragile state of mind that she is in. Although her words are raw, we recognize Cheyanne has come so far. At times she demonstrates her magnificence as she creates new goals and then quickly achieves them. The weight of her grief is a burden, but still she demonstrates her grandeur in flashes. As parents, Kristine and I will do what is necessary to help her continue her healing. We will help her to learn to celebrate not only who she is, how strong she is, but how far she has come and just how magnificent she can be.

Chapter Seventeen

BALANCE AND THE BURDEN

<u>Quinton's Lesson</u>: Dad, you are making great progress!

So many who have read *Quinton's Messages* have connected with the first chapter titled "Found, but Lost Again." In that chapter I recounted that I was always working, commuting to work and, therefore, away from my family for the better part of a decade while living in Colorado. We can't escape the simple fact that the vast majority of us have to work. I mean, we have to earn a decent amount of money so we can live comfortably. The job is a means to an end. The impression you may have is that "the job" was the problem. By July 12, 2013, six months had passed since I resigned from a very nice job. That's when I came to realize that the job wasn't the problem; I WAS, and I still am – at times.

I've had some really great jobs over my entire professional career, from supervising the cleaning crew at the Valley National Bank building in Phoenix, running the family janitorial business in Arizona that we grew to over 400 employees, managing commercial class A office buildings, being responsible for the actions of staff, venders and multimillion dollars in building assets. Through it all, I am honored to have touched so many while improving the value of the buildings I managed. So what was the problem? The jobs were great.

One of my problems was when I arrived home to my wonderful family. For some reason I wasn't completely present with them. It is so easy to blame it on being tired, exhausted and spent or whatever adjective you and I can choose, but that was an excuse. I was good at excuses for not being present with my family, and all of them were bogus. I would get home, and if I wasn't thinking about my day or thinking about what I needed to do tomorrow, I was thinking about what I needed to do next week, month or next year. I wasn't present, and my family suffered. The other problem is I continue to need the job to feel good about myself. I was still trying to be okay after all these years! Call it what you will, perhaps you do the same thing; rely on your job to feel good about yourselves, which is why some struggle with retirement. For me, the solution is so simple, while still unattainable at times. If I remember that God loves me, just the way I am—imperfections and all, I'm fine. I've discovered that the job is the vehicle to provide for myself and our family, not a means of self-esteem. But I didn't know that!

My own shortcomings are opportunities for improvement. The hard part now for me is to stop being filled with regret. Sometimes I find myself failing, now almost six years after Quinton has passed. This is the burden. I do my best to bury it, to tuck it away in the darkness and ignore it while knowing that someday I will have to make peace with this flaw, or at least forgive myself. That's the lesson I'm working on now.

Compounding my regrets is the way I have forgotten so many of the good times Quinton and I enjoyed, and the fun we had together as a family, while being haunted by the times I was not a good father. Isn't that odd? I know I am not alone with this; I have read and heard that many of us are the same way.

We had good times, movie dates, playing catch, shooting baskets, walking to the end of the cul-de-sac to check on the construction of our neighbor's home (Rob and Mindy Johns), watching Knight Rider every Wednesday night, the list goes on. An example of a day I can't shake is the Saturday I went out to run errands and bought lunch for myself, but nothing for the family. When I returned home Quinton was so hurt that silent tears rolled down his cheeks.

Another time he wanted to look through the telescope he received as a Christmas present, when it was well below freezing. I didn't because it was too cold, and I was too tired. What I wouldn't do for a big "do over" on those two occasions. But those are missed opportunities.

Yes, this is my burden, my cross to bear, and I will attempt to bear it by finally learning and then mastering the art of being present. Part of being present is being aware of the momentary failings and never repeating them again. The other part is to learn to forgive myself for those missed opportunities, or to be more honest the times I mess up.

Maybe in remembering the mistakes, but not dwelling on them, we are free to be present and continue to evolve spiritually. This is the blessing. I'm a granddad now and am present with my grandson. My struggles have made me wiser. I share that wisdom with you; learn through the burden that I carry, without having to carry the burden yourself. This is my gift to you, if you choose to accept it.

While it is easy to commit to being present, easier still to merely talk about it amongst ourselves. But as so many of you know, it can be next to impossible to achieve. I know. I struggled with it for a decade, the entirety of Quinton's life. While I knew I was out of balance and was committed to becoming balanced, each year it was worse. How many of you struggle with this? While I envy those of you who have mastered the balance and the being present, I empathize with the masses who haven't.

For those struggling as I did, I invite you to put yourself in my shoes. For a moment, imagine your son or daughter dying. One of the blessings is that some of you may, through imagining going through such a nightmare, wake up and begin to **appreciate what you have**. Yes, this is a blessing, and it is yours!

Tomorrow is not promised. It is reality that dying is part of living. None of us are immune from it, so why ignore it and assume that it always happens to other folks? It matters not if you are rich or poor, yellow, red, brown, black or white; death will arrive at your doorstep at an unexpected time.

Understanding this fact helps provide additional impetus to be present with your loved ones. Perhaps, but if it does, it is only for a relative moment. The push and pull of our busy lives will invariably pull the wool over our eyes again and leave us unappreciative of life, our loved ones, our good health, and the simple yet abundant blessings we have in our lives. At some point, we have to go deeper than merely wanting to have more time with our loved ones or wishing to be in the moment with them. We have to actually address what may be the root problem.

When we turn the television on, surf the web or read the paper, we are bombarded with advertisements for everything–bigger homes, nicer cars, more stuff–and lots of food that really isn't too good for us. So what is wrong with that, you may ask? Nothing in and of itself. The deeper problem is how it affects us. We are conditioned from a very early time in our lives to want it; to want it all and to even feel entitled to the biggest and best our country has to offer.

Often parents, if they have the financial resources, will buy their children all the gadgets they can afford. Sometimes they do this because they feel guilty for being away from them for so long. Even if they can't afford the toys and gadgets for their children, the children see their friends' toys and their want grows even more. As they get older they feel even more entitled to the biggest and best. There is an AT&T commercial on TV that speaks to this programming; that bigger and faster is the only way to go (http://www.youtube.com/watch?v=chgsxK1rSRo). It is a sad state of affairs we find ourselves in.

I suggest that we slow down and enjoy the silence. Let's listen to the whispers – those subtle and quiet voices—the voices of God and Spirit.

But after we are locked into the rut of our lives and often can't fathom a different approach. We think that if we work harder and move faster, we'll climb out of this hole.

So many of us enter adulthood looking for jobs that will earn us the most possible money so we can buy what we think we are supposed to have: the big house, fancy cars and toys galore. Often we take jobs that don't even fulfill us in any way, shape or form; many are miserable in our jobs but feel trapped because we need the big salary to afford the stuff we think we're supposed to have, or to pay for what we've already purchased.

Often both parents have to work long hours to pay the bills; their kids are left to fend for themselves, which is scary because now our society is raising our children. I am talking about what they can find when they surf the net and turn on the TV. This is bad enough, awful in fact, and made worse as parents, trying to compensate for not being there, will substitute love and attention by buying the kids lots of toys and gadgets.

I have discovered that our children don't want the gadgets; they just want and even crave our presence in their lives, at least during the younger portion of their lives. As they grow older, they need our presence in their lives for other reasons, whether they know it or not. They need our loving attention to nurture their souls and guide them – not the TV, Internet or what they see in "the world" to shape their values.

So what's a person to do? First, we all need to consider what it means to live within our means. In today's age, that statement is almost counter intuitive and maybe even un-American. For many it is becoming an economic necessity to downsize, living more simply; grandparents, grown children and parents are living under one roof. More and more of this is happening in our great country; my family included.

You may think I am taking the concept of living within our means to an extreme, but it is happening nevertheless. "Per results of a study by Pew Research Center in 2010 approximately 50 million (nearly one in six) Americans, including rising numbers of seniors, live in households with at least two adult generations and often three. It has become an ongoing trend for elderly generations to move in and live with their children, as they can give them support and help with everyday living" (Wikipedia: Cherlin, Andrew J., *Public and Private families*, McGraw Hill, 2010).

Some who embark on this path may initially feel like a failure, yet soon they begin to see that it is a viable solution, and the benefits are many. With that said, it won't be easy. Grandparents may find themselves back in a parenting role, and now young parents feel as if they are children again. Even though beneficial, this arrangement takes hard work; primarily by the grandparents to ensure that within this extended family, their kids have the space to work through their own issues, continuing on their individual journeys of spiritual growth.

This model for a family isn't revolutionary. Look to the past, study history and you will see it used to be the normal family, not only in these United States of America but even further back. The Native American family structure also included the grandparents in the core family unit, and for good reason. To hunt and gather took a whole community. These functions took the able-bodied young adults and both parents. Sounds like today's culture, yes?

While the able-bodied young adults gathered the necessities to keep the family fed and sheltered, the kids were left on their own; only they weren't. The eldest and wisest not only took care of them, but also taught them everything they would need to know to function successfully in society and enjoy life. The grandparents taught the kids.

The distinctive work of the grandparents is that of acquainting the children with the traditions and beliefs of the nation. The grandparents are old and wise. They had lived and achieved. They are dedicated to the service of the young, as their teachers and advisers, and the young in turn regard them with love and reverence. In them the Indian recognizes the natural and truest teachers of the child. It is reserved for them to repeat the time-hallowed tales with dignity and authority, so as to lead the child in the inheritance of the stored-up wisdom and experience of the race (The Wisdom of the Native Americans, New World Library, pages 102-103, 1999).

I am sure you see the parallel. This same family model is customary throughout the world in the past and present. "In many cultures, such as those of many of the Asians, Middle Easterners, Africans, Eastern Europeans, Indigenous Latin Americans and Pacific Islanders, *extended families* are the basic family unit. Even in Western Europe, extended families were also clearly prevalent" (Wikipedia, Family Types and the Persistence of Regional Disparities in Europe).

When we learn to live within our means, the proverbial less is more approach, trying to achieve work-life balance may actually become an achievable goal. We must be aware of the temptation to be present for a moment, but lose it when the pressure increases from trying to complete all of the work requirements. The temptation is there because of work requirements that, in some professions, will never be totally completed, even if you worked 16 hours a day.

Seems like we should be able to figure this out and many are. There is so much at stake; our future is at stake and that of our children. Our children are our future, and somehow we need to change our priorities as a country from amassing wealth to educating our children to be ambassadors for the planet. A vital goal, but we can do whatever we put our minds to. We have done it before, and we can do it again.

Chapter Eighteen

SO, WHAT'S THE POINT OF A LIFETIME?

Quinton's Lesson: All of life has purpose!

Another blessing from the awful tragedy of losing our son in the physical realm is that we now *know* we exist on the other side. Quinton has shown us, and for many of you, your deceased loved ones have shown you. How, you may ask, is this a blessing? The blessing is in knowing that we, too, exist on the other side, which puts our lifetime here into a different context.

There is meaning for each of us in our lives. I dare say that in every tragedy, every heartbreak, every struggle, every moment of emotional distress, there is an opportunity to learn and grow in some way. I can say this because of what we experienced firsthand. As we have said, we felt the accident that took our son's life was preordained, and we felt it coming – like it was lurking over our shoulders during the week before Quinton's death.

On some level, maybe on a spiritual plane, we knew change was coming but didn't know exactly what that meant. And then, I look at the effect on our lives and the lives of others who have been deeply impacted by what happened to us. I realize the impact is largely a positive one. Many have become more balanced in their lives, more appreciative of their loved ones and even look at their own lives in a different context. So many of us have been further enlightened and inspired because of what Quinton helped us to see. This is especially true for me. ***From this*** *perspective, it seems the purpose of Quinton's life was to help many of us.*

I look at my own life of risk taking, where my life was in jeopardy time and time again. Each time I was spared. Then as I matured, I became less reckless only to lose my son in an accident, an accident that Kristine and I should have died in while Quinton should have survived. This is my context; my lifetime and experiences.

Surviving the accident that took our son's life and surviving the dangerous driving of my youth cannot be chalked up to chance. The purpose of my life is not to climb into a bottle or check out for the rest of my time here. From that perspective, the reason I am here becomes a little less murky. And the same goes for all of us as you, too, have your own individual purpose(s). So how do we know what our purpose is?

In my life I look at my own reoccurring cycles and what I have struggled with during my life. When I say struggles, I am speaking about pain of some sort. It might be emotional hurts, physical pain or even spiritual pain, and it keeps reoccurring in my life. For the most part, I have been dealing with my reoccurring cycles, which I have come to consider opportunities for improvement, by employing the same coping mechanisms. My coping mechanisms have had very little to do with addressing my personal root issues. They say the definition of insanity is doing the same thing over and over, but expecting a different result each time. Maybe you can see where I am going with this. So, what am I here to learn?

My sincere hope is that in sharing some of my own struggles as honestly as I can, it may help you to look at your life in a similar way and identify your own opportunities for growth.

In my life, I have and continue to struggle with a myriad of things. Maybe the single largest issue is I am not in touch with my emotions. I have coping mechanisms that I have employed over the years when I am unable to process what I am feeling, resulting from being stressed out, under pressure or hurting in some way. Often I turn to food as a way to swallow my emotions and another, lifting weights in the gym. Eating too much and lifting weights may have worked on a shallow level as a younger man, but now, not so much.

My metabolism has slowed, I have a bad knee from the accident and a bad shoulder from football. If I eat too much it is a great deal more difficult to burn it off; and when I lift, usually I end up trying to lift too much. At this point, usually causing me more pain than benefit. When these two coping mechanisms are employed in tandem, I actually gain weight, end up feeling sluggish, with a belly too big and have set myself up to have a heart attack or some other ailment. Still, I turn to these coping mechanisms because it is what I know.

This is a very superficial example of what I am talking about. This is but one of my reoccurring cycles, and the only result of utilizing these coping mechanisms is some short-term relief from my inner turmoil. Yet I have done absolutely nothing to resolve it, only momentarily numbing the pain. My inner turmoil is my reoccurring cycle and a constant reminder. Herein is an opportunity for me to learn something. One of the purposes of my life is to begin more fully, experiencing my emotions instead of swallowing them.

The reoccurring cycle is something that keeps happening over the years and continues to cause us some level of pain, whether it be emotional or physical. It triggers us to become stressed or hurt or lonely or depressed, and we turn to our coping mechanism of choice expecting or hoping that this time it may actually work while knowing it has never worked before. A coping mechanism can be any number of things, like over indulging in alcohol, food, marijuana or some other drug, or sitting in front of the TV for hours or shopping for unnecessary things – anything to numb the pain we find ourselves in. Doing this over and over is the definition of insanity, an insanity that I know all too well!

Sometimes I find myself in a place where I don't feel good about myself. During my last round of coping, I gained weight, injured my surgically repaired shoulder and often was in physical pain. I know it doesn't work long term, so I am trying to find the courage, resolve and focus to try something different.

I plan to meditate more, go outside and walk or bike ride instead of going inside to lift weights. My desire is to break the reoccurring cycle; to do something different and more to the point, set my intention to embrace my emotions. I am happy to say that I am beginning to feel; I am crying more often and I am grateful to do so. It is nice to express the emotion of sadness or grief. For that matter, it is has been nice to express a broad range of the emotions that I have been keeping inside for so much of my life.

All right, now let's go a little deeper.

About a year ago, I turned to my wife Kristine and said, "Here it is again, just like when I was 21 years old." At that point in my life, I had broken away from the financial security my father provided; I was sick and tired of the volatility, and living in fear. My anger toward our family situation and anger at feeling helpless in the past was only beginning to show its face. I was beginning to grow up and chart my own path. I was beginning to think and build professional relationships that I felt would be mutually beneficial in the not-too-distant future.

Then my father called, saying he needed my help with the business he started. He knew how to play me like a fiddle. If anyone asked me for help at that point in my life, I had a hard time turning away. To the point, though, I had a choice. Run home to papa (translation--take the easy way) or continue to struggle with charting my own path and finding my own way. Well, I took the less challenging path. It has been quite a journey, and I believe the intended path, but it was the easier path at that point in time.

Quinton's Legacy

As of the writing of this book, I find myself in the same place. Do I take the less challenging path or the more challenging path? Interestingly, the context of the question has changed. I have come to realize it has less to do with what is most challenging and more to do with how I can engage my family on a deeper level while being engaged with life. I am just starting to reach this deeper level. From that perspective, another purpose of my life is to learn the lesson that I can face any challenge and not lose myself in it. **Simply stated, the core of my journey is to learn that I am loved and can embody love, even while standing in the fire.**

While I realize the example above doesn't have to be black and white, I hope you understand my point. I am breaking a reoccurring cycle in my life! I can choose to challenge myself or not. While choosing to challenge myself professionally, can I be engaged with my own family at the same time? In the context of my life, the choice is simple. I will not lose sight of what is most important no matter how busy I am at work. I chose family, Quinton's gift to me, in a manner of speaking. My choices are to keep doing the same thing while expecting different results, or branch off into rarified air by trying something different to me. My suggestion is that if what you are doing is causing you pain, then change it!

What is your reoccurring cycle? Do you keep finding yourself in destructive relationships, with a person who verbally puts you down or worse, beats you down? Many folks don't feel worthy of a relationship with someone who can lift them up and grow with them. Break the cycle by first knowing you are worthy of a good relationship, then look for the kind of person who won't tear you down. Do you cheat yourself by selling your soul for a dollar every time the going gets tough? Next time, go ahead and take the honest job even if it means cleaning toilets or flipping burgers; keep your integrity intact by not lying or cheating. Earn the money honestly.

Let's go deeper still.

The point of a reoccurring cycle is to give us an opportunity for spiritual growth. It is an opportunity to overcome terror, addictions, being selfish, rude or living life in a fearful manner. I very recently became aware of yet another one of my reoccurring cycles: facing fear. I've mentioned my rocky relationship with my father, which included having him pull a gun on me, pointing it between my eyes. More recently, an insight came as a result of working with a difficult client.

During the course of a recent job, I had a difficult client who alternated between being very sweet and being very demanding, and at times, nasty. I was tasked with working with this client and even welcomed the challenge. Over the course of months, I began to realize that I was having a physical reaction in dealing with this situation. I noticed my throat and chest got tight, my voice changed and my heart actually raced.

The surprise was that when it got to that point, I remembered that it had happened before; all those years that I had struggled with my father. This certainly qualifies as a reoccurring cycle in my life and provides me with another opportunity! In facing this cycle, I realized that I have yet to be completely okay with myself and still need to work on dealing with my emotions. I can choose to be disappointed in myself – that these are still issues – or I can be grateful that I have yet another opportunity to deal with my underlying issue. I choose the later!

Not long after, I was speaking into my recorder, to process what I shared above and had something of an epiphany. As I spoke to my spiritual guide, to Quinton and to God, I had an astonishing realization. A gentle whisper told me, "It is like being in the lion's dens." Was I in the lion's den, facing insurmountable odds in this life? Another life? Facing defeat, facing death? Is this similar to that feeling of letting someone down, letting myself down or feeling like a complete failure? While it's a little challenging to connect the dots here, I do know it is my cycle, and face it I will. After all, I am okay and God does love me. **By being aware**

of the cycle, I can glimpse the larger picture and begin understanding what it is I am supposed to learn.

There are so many reoccurring cycles we face as individuals. Mine relate to learning how to express my emotions instead of swallowing them, learning that I am loved, always; and simply learning to have faith that it will all work out as long as I keep applying myself. Think about your reoccurring cycles. Discover and acknowledge them. In doing so, begin to understand what it is you would learn if you dealt with them differently; if you tried a completely different approach. In looking at your pain, struggles and your own cycles this way, you may discover what your purpose is. Life is better once you break through, but if you chose not too, that is okay. There is always your next lifetime to try again. But wait, we are here now. Why not embrace the opportunity now? Why not break the cycle now? Why not learn that you are worthy now and stop settling for destructive relationships and break the addictions–NOW!

We are here now. Why not overcome the tendency of being arrogant, prideful and or judgmental? These are coping mechanisms too! Why not learn to be more humble, gentle and loving? Why not learn to be less self-centered and narcissistic if you are too self-centered and narcissistic?

Figure out your reoccurring cycle, forgive yourself for being imperfect and then take the opportunity to work through it. And when you stumble, forgive yourself again, for neither you nor I are perfect. Try again and again and again. It is okay. NOW is all we have. Keep forgiving yourself and keep moving forward. You will be successful. Have faith in yourself!

Chapter Nineteen

REINCARNATION

Quinton's Lesson: Learning may take unexpected turns; don't be afraid of where it leads you!

In *Quinton's Messages* I spoke around the subject of reincarnation but did not discuss it directly. I know it is a divisive and galvanizing topic, although maybe not as much as it used to be 20 or 30 years ago. We referred to Quinton and others as old souls, but we only alluded to reincarnation as a possibility. My belief about the fabric of our existence would be missing a key puzzle piece if I didn't include this topic. I'm happy to share what I know.

When we look at the world today and see how so many struggle, how so many suffer through, seemingly destroying their lives and the lives of others, it really is hard for me to think we only get one chance at life. It just doesn't make sense. I look at my own struggles, seemingly born with them. As we walk through life, we see those who are truly wise, gentle and have such a calming energy, versus those of us who just thrash about in our lives. Why does that happen?

When I was a young man in school, the conversation about who we are centered on "nature vs. nurture." Today, that just doesn't explain the difference that I can see within my own family, and it certainly does not explain today's children. There is something else going on.

Look at all the needless and meaningless deaths of so many throughout history and within our lifetime. Knowing that we exist on the other side; knowing that the death of the body isn't really the death of the soul, changes my view of their deaths. Consider the possibility that they come back with the opportunity to live a different life. For those of us who are parents who have lost children to death, what is the point?

Many of us parents are fortunate enough to recognize our transitioned children as old souls, sent here to not only bless us with their presence, but also to help us learn something or improve in some way. How are children recognized as old souls without reincarnation?

When Quinton transitioned back to pure energy, the most amazing epiphany was to realize that he still exists. That knowledge put me on a path of study. Investigating spiritual topics is something most of us don't take the time to do. When I set out, I had absolutely no idea that my search would encompass the topic of reincarnation, but I found lots of information about it.

Through it all, there is nothing more powerful than the testimony of a young child before corrupted by the world today and that of someone who was once a skeptic. Brian Weiss, M.D., was such a skeptic, and his testimony regarding reincarnation is exceptionally potent. Dr. Weiss was a very well-educated medical doctor who established his career in psychiatry based upon a very main stream view of life and medicine. His hard work and dedication to his craft led to greater and greater success, leading to him becoming very well regarded in his field. He ended up publishing 37 scientific papers and book chapters as he became even more respected for his experience and opinions. In his first book, published in 1988, Dr. Weiss explains his background immediately in the preface: "Years of disciplined study had trained my mind to think as a scientist and physician, molding me along the narrow paths of conservatism in my profession. I distrusted anything that could not be proved by traditional scientific methods."

Quinton's Legacy

Dr. Weiss was a traditional western medicine-oriented doctor. While he was aware of the studies in parapsychology, they seemed too farfetched and did not hold his attention. And then he met Catherine in approximately 1983, and his view of the world and life in general changed forever! After 18 months of treating Catherine with conventional psycho-therapy, he decided to try a technique a little bit off the reservation.

He tried hypnosis. While she was under hypnosis, he asked her to go back to a time where a particular symptom was manifested. He was blown away by the results; as Catherine went back to when certain symptoms began, she began sharing previous lives, 86 of them to be exact, over the following 12 months. Lifetimes as a man and woman, lifetimes where she had blonde hair, brown hair or an afro; lifetimes as a soldier, student, servant, destitute, outcast and well off.

As the lifetimes were shared, the symptoms, phobias and issues she had dealt with her entire life subsided, and many of them quickly. The good doctor sat on this information, not sharing it publically for four years because he was afraid of what his colleagues would say–afraid that he would become an outcast among his peers for disclosing his discovery. He discovered that we do reincarnate and, for at least some of us, often.

Finally, in 1988, he published *Many Lives, Many Masters* and has published many more books since. He was compelled to share the truth, even if doing so destroyed his reputation, career and livelihood. That is a powerful testimony. He stood in the glare of skeptics and possible ridicule, but many in his profession applauded him because they had had similar experiences with their patients while under hypnosis.

The testimony of a child on such matters is equally if not more powerful. A child without motive or conditioning is just sharing what he sees. One example is Colton Burpo in the book, *Heaven is for Real.*

He told about his meeting with Christ during his near death experience, saw both his grandfather and sister, who he'd never met in his young life.

Little Colton's experiences on the other side during a Near Death Experience (NDE) speak to the reality of Christ. Many report that we continue to exist after "death" looking the way we did when we were 30 years old. It further shows that even miscarried children exist on the other side. While this does not prove reincarnation, Colton's testimony is another piece of the puzzle in understanding that a life goes on longer than a "lifetime," as we have been taught. From that larger perspective it is pertinent.

The book *Soul Survivor* by Bruce and Andrea Leininger speaks to reincarnation and in a big way. I was introduced to this story not long after our grandson was born. One afternoon, Cheyanne and I, with little Salvador Quinton sleeping nearby, started watching a program on TV about reincarnation. The program included a story of a small boy named James Leininger. James was two years old when he began having nightmares, actually waking himself up screaming, "Plane on fire! Little man can't get out!" Subsequently the family wrote a book titled *Soul Survivor,* which is described here:

> The centerpiece of a loving family of three, James was a happy, playful toddler who had only just begun stringing together sentences. Determined to understand what was happening to their son, Bruce and Andrea set off on a journey of discovery that was to rock them to their core. For the more they researched the arcane comments and fragmented details little James revealed, the more they were drawn inescapably to a shocking conclusion: that James was reliving the life of James Huston, a World War II fighter pilot who was killed in the battle of Iwo Jima—over sixty years ago!
>
> Through painstaking research and conversations with war veterans and surviving members of James Huston's family, Bruce and Andrea were forced to confront their skepticism

and reexamine their entire belief system. In the process, they not only managed to solve the mystery of their son's statements. They also uncovered revelations about James Huston's life and wartime experiences that could finally bring peace and healing to his loved ones, decades after his death.

Check out this book or simply go to YouTube and search "James Leininger reincarnation" or "Soul Survivor." You will be blown away. Part of their journey was a journey of skepticism; Bruce was skeptical and began this journey of discovery in an effort to disprove any thought that his son was a reincarnated World War Two fighter pilot. With thorough research, he ended up proving it was real. Check it out for yourself.

Reincarnation is referred to on more than one occasion in the New Testament. I found a couple of passages myself as I read the New Testament for the first time within two years of Quinton's transition, and it immediately caught my eye. I am sure reading the work of Dr. Michael Newton and Dr. Brian Weiss prior to reading the New Testament made it possible for me to notice the passages firsthand.

Roman Emperor Constantine made Christianity the official religion of the Roman Empire in 325 A.D. and commissioned a group of men called the Council of Nicaea with the daunting task of selecting which holy books that had been written by holy men would be included in the Bible and which would not. When you read some of the scriptures that didn't make the cut, you will understand that reincarnation was clearly accepted by Christians at that time, not unlike the Eastern religions. However, when the Council finished with their work, the impression was that Christianity is one of the few religions that doesn't believe in reincarnation. During the course of finalizing the Bible's 58 books, almost all references to reincarnation were removed. Almost. In Malachi 4:5 it is written, "Behold, I will send you Elijah the prophet before the coming of the great and dreadful day of the LORD." Elijah, well-known in the Old Testament, was supposed to return before the Messiah, yet Jesus is widely accepted as that Messiah, our Lord, by the entire Christian world. When Jesus was asked about the prophecy, he faced it head on and in a matter-of-fact manner by replying, "Elijah is indeed coming first to get everything ready. But I tell you Elijah has already come, but he wasn't recognized and they chose to abuse him. Then the disciples realized he was talking about John the Baptist," Matthew 17:10-13. Well, I don't know about you, but to me it sounds like Jesus was describing the reincarnation of Elijah and his return as John the Baptist.

As I continue to read and study, I am amazed at all of the information available for us to devour, for the purpose of shaping our own thoughts about history and our individual place in the world. Recently I came across a book titled *Why Jesus Taught Reincarnation* by Dr. Herbert Bruce Puryear. It is a wonderful book, and I suggest you read it if you are interested in learning more on the topic.

Dr. Puryear is a Christian and a minister, and he uses scripture to support his assertion. In the introduction (page seven) of his book, he answers his own question, "*Where is reincarnation taught?* When we accept the fact that Jesus taught reincarnation, and when we adopt a view of the nature of humankind adequate to the facts, then we will see reincarnation throughout the Bible. It is replete with direct and indirect references to reincarnation. It is not a matter of *reading it in*. It's there!"

The beautiful thing about scripture, within this place in time where we currently exist, is that it is available to everyone. Any and all of us can read whatever we want, whenever we want and read it again if we so choose – and let the words impact us as they see fit.

Some want to debunk mediums and psychics because they interpret spirit through their own fleshly being, through their own perspective born of a lifetime of associations. Yet we want the same people to take the good word as infallible. Weren't the writers of the accepted 58 books of the Bible (and even the numerous books that were rejected) by the

Council of Nicaea all written by people who were also interpreting Spirit through the flesh?

The interpretations of the good word have undoubtedly changed when translated from Aramaic to Greek and Greek to English. The Aramaic language had approximately 11,000 words and English, before the slang that has been recognized of recent times as words, only has 6,000 words. I'm suggesting that some of the meaning was lost across translations. And through it all, the references to and of reincarnation have survived, and rightfully so!

Chapter Twenty

ADVERSITY

Quinton's Lesson: We all have a choice!

All of us face adversity to one extent or another. Can you imagine living a lifetime without it? I expect not, but let's clarify what adversity means. Adversity can be a minor nuisance or a major hardship. As I discuss adversity, I will be considering all degrees of adversity. It all has a purpose in our lives.

Adversity is the greatest teacher we have on this planet – in this school called planet Earth. Naturally, I didn't understand this or consider this in my younger years when adversity was something to be avoided at all costs. One of the first times this concept really pierced my consciousness, I was sitting in a property management conference in Denver. A very well respected and director level property manager, Lyla Gambo, mentioned adversity in her remarks during a panel discussion. She said something to the effect, "Have you ever made a mistake so bad, so grievous, that you thought you might lose your job?" Many of us nodded thinking of the silly mistakes we have made in our lives, while others had grimmer expressions of the pain mistakes have caused. Lyla then continued by saying, "Those are the mistakes I never made again."

Over the years, Lyla's comments have stayed with me. We can learn from adversity, and I submit, maybe this is the point of adversity. Making a mistake and learning the hard way is like learning not to touch a hot stove after touching it. Adversity can be anything that causes us discomfort, whether that discomfort is emotional, spiritual or physical; each and every time it may be a teaching instrument. The lessons range from learning patience, changing the people we associate with, having the faith that you can accomplish anything if you put your mind to, to simply learning that you are not defined by the adversity you face. That is just the tip of the iceberg. Adversity is different for every individual, as are the lessons to be learned.

Some adversity is of a minor nature, minor in the grand scheme of things. The disappointments, the broken hearts, lost jobs and regrets that all of us have. This adversity is painful. Awful, in fact, when in the middle of it – so awful it can seem impossible to bear. I remember this type of adversity. I saw no purpose in it and only wondered why I had to endure it. I pledged to lock myself away to avoid it forever. Looking back now, it makes more sense that each instance carried something to learn, and an opportunity for my own growth.

But there are other instances of adversity, the kind of adversity that lasts a lifetime. When Quinton transitioned, Kristine and I were propelled down a darker path of adversity – a path so difficult that those who knew us wondered how we endured. This is a different adversity many of us have to endure; some of us eventually learned from it while others didn't, choosing instead to run from it in some way. Our adversity opened up the universe to us while, quite honestly, making us so much stronger as individuals and as a couple.

The key to opening this door was Quinton's visits. His visits showed us that life is eternal. In knowing his life is eternal, we understand that so is ours. As this knowledge began to permeate my consciousness, I was curious as to how it all worked, and how it was that I didn't know prior to Quinton's passing. Thirsty to answer these questions, my studies began – all because of Quinton's transition – all because of adversity. Adversity was my catalyst for change.

Kristine and I have talked with many parents whose children have transitioned. You might be surprised how many of them live joyously, in part because their children have visited them from the other side. Sure, all of us have regrets and frequently have pain in our hearts. But with the knowledge that our children really aren't dead, we take solace in the fact that we will be with them again, and we look at our own lives as a gift.

We know that it could have been one of us who transitioned. Because we didn't, we know that there is something that we have yet to do; something yet to learn, something yet to experience, or somebody to teach, or someone to help cope. This knowledge came about all because of adversity. When I look at our tragedy, our adversity, I am amazed how much we have grown spiritually because of it. Adversity is a teacher.

It is said that God only gives us what we can endure. I look at those who are living with disfigurement, paralysis and mental illness with respect and reverence. The spiritual strength and spiritual maturity they must have to not only live, but to live each day embracing the knowledge that they are making the world a better place by demonstrating their strength and grace to others while learning just how powerful they are. I don't know that I have this strength, yet I trust that I'll be given what I need by God.

Our world community faces even deeper levels of adversity. Too many of our brothers and sisters live with the reality of war and killing for absolutely no reason. We live on a planet where we have been subjecting each other to war for thousands of years – tens of thousands of years according to some historical accounts – and still it goes on today. Why are we afraid of one another? During 2014, 100,000 Jewish citizens of France left the country because of the reemergence of anti-Semitism; why is there still religious hate? What can we learn from this adversity? Maybe it is not to be defined by the attitudes of others.

Some, like Drs. Weiss and Newton, tell us that it is a matter of karma, but not in the way you might think. The karma they speak of isn't about revenge; it is about experience and understanding. In one life a man might perpetuate an injustice. Then to balance the karma, in the next life, a similar injustice is done to that same man. In fully understanding both perspectives, we experience firsthand, the sanctity of a life. We learn what an absolute waste it is to commit injustice to another.

So much of our lives here on this planet are about choice. Life just isn't going to be easy for many of us; *each of us has a choice about how we will react to adversity*. We can be filled with fear, hatred and anger or be filled with joy, gratitude and appreciation. What will you choose?

The choices we make create energy. Being filled with fear, hatred, rage and anger really makes it difficult to find joy and love. Being filled with gratitude and appreciation attracts more of the same to us. Dwelling on the past injustice and letting that energy consume us is not the answer, but understanding the past injustice certainly might help us to stop the cycle. Hatred will not end hatred, and at this point in our history, it no longer matters who started it! What does matter is that soon we will reach a tipping point where enough of us are willing to wipe the slate clean, meet face to face and begin to heal the thousands of years old rifts among us. And when we do, then, collectively, we will begin to heal the human family.

Interestingly, I see progress. I see people with a loving, confident, kindness that permeates the air around them. Many are evolving beyond this dark path, and it is a joy to see. I have met many young people who don't see color, instead only a human being. Many of them do not see socio-economic and religious differences, instead they only seeing other human beings. The fact is, many children and older folks alike are reaching this non-judgmental state of mind, which does illustrate spiritual growth. There is hope for us.

Summary

My desire for you is that both my books, *Quinton's Legacy* and *Quinton's Messages*, inspire you to make the most of your life here and today. Be present in your life, to the best of your ability; be present with your loved ones, your family and true friends. They are your core and your support system. Have fun and enjoy your time here. Enjoy the games, the laughter and being together. Share your wisdom and allow others to share their wisdom with you. None of us here is perfect; all of us have something to share and something to learn.

While telling you tomorrow isn't promised as impetus for being present, it is even more profound than that. My wish is for you to become aware of whatever demons you are dealing with, be it addictions, cruelty, greed, materialism. Why not face them and work through them now?

Our lives take on even greater significance when we embrace the truth that we exist beyond the flesh; that we continue to exist even after our bodies have died, and some of us reincarnate. What we have shared in our two books clearly demonstrates that we exist beyond the flesh. My hope is that this knowledge allows you to look at your lives in a different context. Our lives don't have to be a competition for status, self-esteem or material possessions. We don't have to put others down just to makes ourselves feel good. Our lives have greater purpose than that.

We can take a stand based upon love and compassion against the silliness of the world, and if it costs us a job or a friendship, so be it. If we take a higher perspective of our own individual lives, maybe we can break our reoccurring cycles and come away with something far more valuable. The goal is to make a righteous stand to achieve freedom from a fear-based reality, freedom from being a victim, and the discovery of how magnificent we are.

Make the most of your time here. Be appreciative of every sunrise, every sunset, every smile, every tear and every breath. Be appreciated of every struggle, because each is really an opportunity for something more. Face it head-on. Follow your dreams and be appreciative of everything.

Don't hold on to past regrets or perceived slights by another or even those times when you have done wrong to somebody. You have to forgive yourself and others to move on, to ascend to a better mindset. Try not to surround yourself with negative people or put up with a negative situation just because you are afraid to change. There's no need to try to prove you are strong because at some point, you may become a negative person too.

Try to slow down and really see people. Take the time to see opportunities to make a difference in the lives of others. Try to do it out of the goodness of your heart. If you can't find the goodness in your heart at the moment, fake it and do it just because – until you feel it in your heart. Making a difference in the life of another is a gift, especially if you expect nothing in return. I am fond of saying, "Everyone, no matter whether they are good or bad, gets tapped on the shoulder from time to time and told 'you are up; go and make a difference in that person's life.'"

I wish you all the best.

Afterword

It has now been six years since Quinton's transition. I feel as if I have wandered aimlessly trying to figure out what is next for me, stuck in my mind and not living from my heart. Through it all, I am growing and facing my own opportunities for improvement. I know Quinton is watching over me, urging me on. Little Salvador Quinton is certainly by my side with his own unconditional love, as only a child knows. As I spend time with him, I can't help but think of Quinton and remember to be present with my grandson!

While I would love to change the world, I am going to stay focused on changing myself and pursuing my own peace of mind as I imagine a cabin in the woods with room for my family and friends to visit; one that isn't too far out of the way. And through the remainder of this lifetime, I will continue to write, but don't expect it will be only on spirituality – if I will ever publish again. I write because I have this voice in my head that is incessantly making comments on what is going on in the world. With my perspective on life, what I have come to know with far-ranging interests, it seems like a waste not to share my thoughts via a keyboard. Who knows what may come of that.

I wish you peace and love.

Blessings to you!

BOOKS I HAVE READ SINCE QUINTON WAS CALLED HOME TO HELP ME FIND GREATER UNDERSTANDING:

Proof of Heaven, Eben Alexander, M.D.

Credere, H. L. Balcomb

The Barber's Song, K. Douglas Bassett

Meditation for Dummies, Stephan Bodian

Life on the Other Side, Sylvia Browne

Heaven is for Real, Todd Burpo with Lynn Vincent

Angels in my Hair, Lorna Byrne

The Power of Myth, Joseph Campbell

If You Had an Hour to Live, Richard Carlson and Kristine Carlson

House of Rain, Craig Childs

The Alchemist, Paulo Coelho

People of the Red Earth – American Indians of Colorado, Sally Crum

Lame Deer, Seeker of Visions, Lame Deer and Richard Erodes

Wishes Fulfilled, Dr. Wayne W. Dyer

Embraced by the Light, Betty J. Eadie

Return to the Sacred, Jonathan Ellerby

When Fear Falls Away, Jan Frazier

A Time to Grieve, Kenneth C. Haugk

Experiencing Grief, Kenneth C. Haugk

Finding Hope and Healing, Kenneth C. Haugk

Messages from the Afterlife, Mark Ireland

Soul Shift, Mark Ireland

Dine': A History of the Navajos, Peter Iverson

Quinton's Messages, Ernie Jackson

Last Song, A True Lakota Love Story, Mark Kilburn

Conversations with my Daughter on the Other Side, Barbara B. Lauman

Safe in the Arms of God, John MacArthur

The Instruction: Living the Life Your Soul Intended, Ainslie MacLeod

Life After Life, Raymond A. Moody, Jr., M.D.

Dying to be Me, Anita Moorjani

The Wisdom of the Native Americans, Kent Nerburn

New Testament

Destiny of Souls, Michael Newton, Ph.D.

Journey of Souls, Michael Newton Ph.D.

Memories of the Afterlife, Michael Newton, Ph.D.

HOPI, Susanne & Jake Page

The Gnostic Gospels, Elaine Pagels

90 Minutes in Heaven, Don Piper

Reporting for the Other Side, Tina Powers

Ghosts Among us, James Van Praagh

Growing up in Heaven, James Van Praagh

Talking to Heaven, James Van Praagh

Unfinished Business, James Van Praagh

Stephen Lives, Anne Puryear

Why Jesus Taught Reincarnation, Herbert Bruce Puryear

Celestine Prophecy, James Redfield

Secrets of Shambhala: In Search of the Eleventh Insight, James Redfield

The Celestine Vision: Living a New Spiritual Awareness, James Redfield

The Tenth Insight: Holding the Vision, James Redfield

The Twelfth Insight: Hour of Decision, James Redfield

Spook: Science takes on the Afterlife, Mary Roach

Spirited, Rebecca Rosen

The Atlas of the North American Indian-3rd edition

Your Soul's Plan, Robert Schwartz

The Case for Christ, Lee Strobel

The Ancient Southwest, David E. Stuart

Conversations with God: Book One, Neal Donald Walsch

Conversations with God: Book Two, Neal Donald Walsch

Conversations with God: Book Three, Neal Donald Walsch

Illuminations for a New Era, Suzanne Ward

Mathew, Tell me About Heaven, Suzanne Ward

Revelations for a New Era, Suzanne Ward

Voices of the Universe, Suzanne Ward

The Purpose Driven Life, Rick Warren

Many Lives, Many Masters, Brian L Weiss, M.D.

Messages from the Masters, Brian Weiss, M.D.

Miracles Happen: The Transformational Healing of Past Life Memories, Brian Weiss

Mirrors of Time: Using Regression for Physical, Emotional and Spiritual Healing, Brian L. Weis, M.D.

Only Love is Real: A story of Soul Mates Reunited, Brian Weiss, M.D.

Same Soul, Many Bodies, Brian L Weiss, M.D

Through Time into Healing, Brian Weiss, M.D.

The Shack, Paul Young

AUDIO CDS

The Secret

VIDEOS

The Teachings of Abraham, Ester and Jerry Hicks

The Law of Attraction in Action – Episode I-The Secret Behind the Secret!

The Law of Attraction in Action – Episode II-Keys to Freedom!

The Law of Attraction in Action – Episode III-The Law of Attraction in Action

The Law of Attraction in Action – Episode IV-Chill Out!

The Law of Attraction in Action – Episode V-Revealing the Secret!

The Law of Attraction in Action – Episode VI-Path of Enthusiasm!
The Law of Attraction in Action – Episode VII-Everything You Want!
The Law of Attraction in Action – Episode VIII-Joyous Adventure!
The Law of Attraction in Action – Episode IX-Telling a New Story!
The Law of Attraction in Action–Episode X-Let Loose!
The Law of Attraction in Action–Episode XI-Who You Really Are!
Abraham – Art of Allowing: Death & Life–DVD 8
Abraham – Art of Allowing: Health & Well Being–DVD 9
Beyond the Law of Attraction
The Power of Myth, Joseph Campbell
How great is our God, Louie Giglio
Indescribable, Louie Giglio

MOVIES

Avatar
Charlie St. Cloud
Heaven Is for Real
Hereafter
Inception
Interstellar
If I Stay
Star Wars–A New Hope
The Celestine Prophecy
The Giver
The Matrix
What Dreams May Come
What the Bleep Do we Know!?

BIBLIOGRAPHY

Browne, Sylvia, *Life on the Other Side,* Penguin Putman, Inc., New York, NY, July 2001.

Burpo, Todd, *Heaven is for Real,* Thomas Nelson Inc., Nashville, TN, 2010.

Lewis, C.C., *A Grief Observed,* Harper One, March 3, 2009.

Moorjani, Anita, *Dying to Be Me,* Hay House, Inc., page 74, March 2012.

Nerburn, Kent, *The Wisdom of the Native Americans,* New World Library, March 1999.

New Living Translation 2nd Edition, Tyndale House Publishers, Inc.

Newton, Michael PhD, *Journey of Souls,* Llewellyn Worldwide, Woodbury, MN, 1994.

Rosen, Rebecca, *Spirited,* Harper Collins Publishers, page 22, 2010.

Wikipedia: Cherlin, Andrew J., *Public and Private Families*, McGraw Hill, 2010

Wikipedia: Family Types and the Persistence of Regional Disparities in Europe.

Wilson, Leianne, *Life Shaping Questions: Your Bridge to Shaping the Life you Desire!* Charleston, SC.

ABOUT THE AUTHOR

Ernie Jackson is the eldest of three, born in New Jersey to Ernie and Frances Jackson. After spending the first 12 years there, the family moved to Colorado, which will forever be his sanctuary, even though he's also lived in Arizona. He started his career in the janitorial field, moving from supervisor to president of the family janitorial company in Arizona. The simple philosophy of the Golden Rule, as well as pride in the service being provided, became his highest priority. The same adage carried him into a successful career in commercial property management.

Ernie has been married 23 years to his beautiful wife Kristine. They have two children, Cheyanne and Quinton. Now they are grandparents and loving it. While both Ernie and Kristine are honored to share what they have learned, at this point they are simply enjoying the blessings of each day. They share their experiences and beliefs about life after death with friends, family, as conference keynotes, and with anyone who reaches out to them with the courage to speak about death. Many ask if they are comfortable speaking about their son's transition. Their answer is, "We smile and say, 'Of course. We have written two books on the topic, so please do not feel uncomfortable asking. We are honored to share.'"

An Ongoing Dialogue Invitation

We would love to hear from you after reading Quinton's Legacy, especially those experiences you have had with your deceased loved ones making contact with you. We offer a safe place for you to share your experiences. Too often, many are reluctant to acknowledge those magical signs and visits because others might not be receptive. Well, we live in a time where more and more are accepting of these experiences. Share them with us without fear of judgment or ridicule. Doing so will benefit you and, with your permission, we will share these experiences in blogs, on Facebook, or in the Helping Parents Heal website.

One of our greatest joys is speaking to groups about our experiences, so please contact us if you have a desire for us to speak with your group about our experiences and how they have changed our views on life. We do keynote presentations and, while tailoring them to the needs of the organization, we offer three basic themes: The **work life balance**, Proof that **life is eternal**, and **how life changes** through the knowledge that life is eternal.

For More Information, contact Ernie or Kristine Jackson:

www.quintonsmessages.com
Ernie
ernie@quintonsmessages.com
Kristine
kristine@quintonsmessages.com

Made in the USA
San Bernardino, CA
14 June 2017